17 Women
WHO SHOOK THE WORLD

Learn the Secrets for Embracing
Highly Effective Lives

A 24-step Program for Achieving
Your Dreams

Schiffer Publishing Ltd

4880 Lower Valley Road • Atglen, PA 19310

Preethi Burkholder

Other Schiffer Books by the Author:
Ghost Towns of the Rockies, 978-0-7643-3569-3, $16.99

Other Schiffer Books on Related Subjects:
Courageous Women of Maryland, 978-0-7643-3541-9, $19.99

Designed by Danielle D. Farmer
Type set in Edwardian Script ITC/Helvetica Neue Lt Pro

ISBN: 978-0-7643-4141-0
Printed in the United States of America

Published by Schiffer Publishing, Ltd.
4880 Lower Valley Road
Atglen, PA 19310
Phone: (610) 593-1777; Fax: (610) 593-2002
E-mail: Info@schifferbooks.com

For the largest selection of fine reference books on this and related subjects, please visit our website at:
www.schifferbooks.com.
You may also write for a free catalog.

This book may be purchased from the publisher.
Please try your bookstore first.

We are always looking for people to write books on new and related subjects. If you have an idea for a book, please contact us at **proposals@schifferbooks.com**

Schiffer Books are available at special discounts for bulk purchases for sales promotions or premiums. Special editions, including personalized covers, corporate imprints, and excerpts can be created in large quantities for special needs. For more information contact the publisher.

In Europe, Schiffer books are distributed by
Bushwood Books
6 Marksbury Ave.
Kew Gardens
Surrey TW9 4JF England
Phone: 44 (0) 20 8392 8585; Fax: 44 (0) 20 8392 9876
E-mail: info@bushwoodbooks.co.uk
Website: www.bushwoodbooks.co.uk

Dedication

I am grateful to all the women and men who believed in me. I thank
you, God, for giving me the motivation to rise after every fall.

To Nancy

With Best Wishes
from the Author
Preeth Burkholder 1/13/13

This book is about individuals gaining control of their destiny and empowering themselves to find success in their lives. Uncover the triumphs, failures, hopes, and disappointments of **17 Women Who Shook the World** who are truly some of the world's most talented and hard-working women. Here you will find athletes, scholars, scientists, humanitarians, and activists of all kinds. All they have in common is their gender.

The anthropologist Margaret Mead said: "Never doubt that a small group of thoughtful committed citizens can change the world; indeed, it's the only thing that ever did." This book examines the lifestyles of women who found success and who made great strides for many of us. These seventeen women were determined to shake the world and make it more pleasant for the majority.

I believe this book speaks to every woman and man. Its message is transcultural. Successful women are everywhere, past and present. They have won Nobel prizes, served on Supreme Courts, led slaves to freedom, raised beautiful families, became billionaires, and will become future trillionaires. Through effort and determination, they have overcome countless challenges to lead successful lives. Some became famous. Most did not. Yet, the unsung heroes were successful in their own ways. To become successful is not merely to get your name published online or in a book or magazine. It is how you feel inside of you.

This book unfolds the life stories of seventeen individuals who changed the world through their vision, courage, determination, and patience. Their stories reveal their struggles as world changers against obstacles such as poverty, financial struggles, discrimination, violence, and injustice. Their stories also tell of their struggles as women to overcome the belief, which still exists in most societies, that girls are less capable than boys of achieving high goals and that women are less likely than men to become leaders. These world-shaking women often needed even more vision and courage than their male counterparts, because as women they faced greater discrimination and resistance. They certainly needed more determination and patience, because no matter how much they proved themselves, there were always people who were reluctant to take their leadership and their achievements seriously, simply because they were women.

However, these challenges did not stop the women included in this book from making their mark in their fields. As they fought, they found inspiration in women as well as men; in their own mothers and grandmothers, and the great women who had come before them. Today, they themselves stand as an inspiration to women and men all over the world.

Most of the seventeen women featured here were born with more disadvantages than you or I can imagine. So, what is it that made them overcome their vicissitudes and become great? What is stopping you from achieving that same level of greatness?

Here is the answer: Each and every one of them made a decision. Yes, that is all it took — an internal decision that manifested externally. Rather than continuing to lead passive, unexamined lives, they decided to lead deliberate, examined lives.

If you are unhappy with where you are in your life today, it is not going to change automatically by tomorrow morning. You have to do something about it. It all starts with a decision. There comes a point when each and every one of us have to make decisions on our own, where we have no "crutch" to lean on. Those are scary times; times of isolation and despair. They are also times of growth. Decisions help us to cross that threshold which transports us to greater things.

However, this book is not just about these remarkable women. It is also about unlocking your dreams and letting them out into the world, thus allowing them to be as big as they were meant to be. The more you dream, the more you will fall in love with yourself and your life. You will be irresistible to the very person who needs to love you the most: You.

Your dreams are yours to cherish. Dreams do come true, if you believe hard enough, work hard enough, and focus hard enough. This book will reprogram how you think about your dreams so that they become real. To be truly happy and inspired by the life you are living, you can take steps to wake up and launch your dreams right now. Some woman out there will burst open and be recognized for achieving success and enjoying the fruits of her dreaming. It might as well be you.

Every woman comes from a different place. Some are content with where they are in life and have no desire to change their predicament. Good for them. Life has turned out just like they want it to, or even better. Others live in fear that there is no other way to live life and so find some peace with the less-than-satisfactory lifestyles that they have been saddled with or, in some cases, the lifestyles they have created for themselves.

The majority of women, however, live in an unsettled state. They are seeking career changes, contemplating the marriages or partnerships they may be in, hanging by a thread financially, or living in denial and quiet desperation as they keep a secret that is crippling them internally everyday. Others feel like their brains are about to blow out because they are carrying so much emotional, financial, and physical weight in their lives.

Most of our limits are self-imposed. Our limits are woven so tightly into the fabric of our being that they have become our truth. If you can remove and observe them, you may find that they are not really a part of you. Rather, they are parasites you have allowed to come along for the free ride. They were probably glued on to you by someone else, including parents, siblings, teachers, bosses, friends, the media, and our own assumptions. The time has come to take these parasites to a "cleaning station," just like fish underwater do.

Observe your associations. You are the company that you keep. Are your associations supporting you in reaching your goals or sucking the energy out of your life? The first step toward cleaning up is acknowledging what needs to be thrown out. Associating with negative people is a sure way to crush your dreams. Negativity is toxic. Negative people make sure that their negativity and pessimism impose a damper on your dreams also. Negative places and negative people can drain anyone's spirit. Associate with people who can lift you higher.

Have perseverance and confidence in yourself. Yes, you can aspire for things sublime. You were born to do something, to be someone. You are never too young, never too old. Don't let anyone stand in your way.

Every woman selected for this book had some talent, no matter how insignificant it seemed. They capitalized on that talent. Victoria Woodhull, for example, claimed she could talk to the dead and that she could get into a trance. She used this skill to predict a stock tip to Cornelius Vanderbilt, the richest man in America at the time, which helped her to finance her presidential campaign in 1872.

If you have reached a level of success, I dare you to go to the next level. You never want to stop looking forward to the next interesting thing. Each woman in this book never stopped contributing to society. That was their greatest asset. Nearly all of the women selected for this book took their pain to help others. Harriet Tubman, for example, took her pain as a slave to help other slaves to find freedom.

Get rid of the myth that you need money to become successful. Money is a great servant, but a lousy master. Most of these women came from financially strapped backgrounds. Some of them were malnourished as children, had no or very little schooling, and led lifestyles far removed from any kind of luxury. When Marie Curie was small, her parents rented out their apartment to students. At one time there were ten boys living there. Space was so tight that Marie had to sleep on the couch. At her apartment close to The Sorbonne, the cold was so intense that at night she had to pile on everything she had in the way of clothing just so she could sleep. Despite these financial difficulties, Marie Curie did not let money get in the way of her success.

Oftentimes, it seems easier to give up or find the easy way out. Yet, strong women persist. Aung San Suu Kyi is a woman who stands for the truth, which seems weak to those who try to oppress her. Here is a woman who could have chosen the easier path and looked the other way, rather than following the path of attempting to take Burma to democratic freedom. Yet, she has followed the truth.

Be true to yourself. To think independently and to stand on one's feet is to think for oneself and to do what is right. Too many women waste their lives trying to be well liked that they forget about adding value. Being a people pleaser can be emotionally exhausting. Forget about living your entire lives trying to make others happy. You can never make everyone else happy. It is humanly impossible. What's more, forget about trying to feel like a victim and getting everyone to feel sorry for you. It helps no one.

Every woman featured here had amazing fortitude to overcome their difficulties. Mother Teresa lost her father when she was eight, Madam C.J. Walker lost both her parents before she was seven, and Esther Morris was an orphan by the time she was ten. The lack of parental guidance did not prevent them from making seismic shifts in this world.

Successful women are determined to achieve what others said they would not be able to do. They do the unthinkable. Wilma Rudolph contracted polio when she was five years old. She was told she would never be able to walk again. Wilma beat all odds and became the fastest woman on earth, winning three Gold medals at the 1960 Olympics.

Successful people leave their flawed past behind and start anew. The following parable illustrates the challenge and the value of letting go of the past.

Two monks were strolling by a stream on their way home to the monastery. They were startled by the sound of a young woman in a bridal gown, sitting by the stream, crying softly. Tears rolled down her cheeks as she gazed across the water. She needed to cross it to get to her wedding, but she was fearful that doing so might ruin her beautiful handmade gown.

In this particular sect, monks were prohibited from touching women, but one monk was filled with compassion for the bride. Ignoring the sanction, he hoisted the woman on his shoulders and carried her across the stream, assisting her journey and saving her gown. She smiled and bowed with gratitude as the monk splashed his way across the stream to rejoin his companion.

The second monk was livid. "How could you do that?" he scolded. "You know that we are forbidden to touch a woman, much less pick one up and carry her around!"

The other monk listened in silence to the stern lecture. The reprimanding lasted all the way back to the monastery. After returning to the monastery, he fell asleep for a few hours. He was awakened in the middle of the night by his fellow monk.

"How could you carry that woman?" the agitated monk cried out. "Someone else could have helped her across the stream. You failed as a monk."

"What woman?" the sleepy monk inquired.

"Don't you even remember? That woman you carried across the stream," the angry monk snapped.

"Oh, her," laughed the sleepy monk. "I only carried her across the stream. You carried her all the way back to the monastery."

The message of this parable is simple: When it comes to our flawed past, leave it at the stream.

What would you do differently today if yesterday never took place? What if you never met that person who remains clouded in your memory? What if you never met with that accident that took your leg? What if you never got that job that made you move to a new country? What if you never said those hurtful things to your relative who is now six feet under?

Many live in the past because they want to be in the victim mode. They want everyone else to feel sorry for them. Being a victim is a craving for attention. The sooner you can get out of victim mode and into architect mode, the higher your likelihood of becoming a successful person.

Many of you have reason to be angry about yesterday. You may have been treated unfairly, cheated of your rightful place, robbed of your trust, denied an inheritance, and blamed for another's misery. Exploring options through the screen of bitterness and anger, however, only blocks the path of success from your life. It does not unravel the path to success. Your judgment is clouded and your energy becomes negative. Your past will take you nowhere. Focus on the future. Holding on to resentment is like clinging on to a hot piece of charcoal in your hand. You are only burning yourself. Clinging on to yesterday has broken the souls of many.

It is time to move on. Say goodbye to the package that has been crippling you internally. This may include people who may have been pulling you back, the opinion others have of you, and past events that may have crippled you. Leaving your past behind is a part of moving forward. Clean your mind. Take the good with you and leave the rest behind. It is a "twist" that needs to be adjusted, mentally, in order for new things to manifest externally. Start anew.

Successful people leave their past and become architects of their own future. Allow that new dam of sunshine to burst through and you will unravel an unlimited list of possibilities pouring out. It is impossible to chart a course in a new direction or make any changes in your life until you know where you are.

No one or no incident can keep us down unless we let them. Sometimes, all it takes is a side remark to steer us off our course. It may have been a comment made by someone in school when you were twelve years old, a cousin who said you would never succeed, or an incident that you witnessed twenty years ago that is still keeping you in the darkness.

Leaving yesterday behind requires a healing of your past. Shoving your past under the rug and pretending it never happened only creates deep-seated resentment that will surface in your new life. You can't change the past. You can, however, come to terms with it and let it go. Until you deal with your past, you are literally dragging the weight of your past into your present. That makes it hard to move forward. Not dealing with your past in healthy ways can steer your focus from productive to destructive. You have to face it in order to erase it. Holding on to the past removes and masks the true potential inherent within.

You can custom design your unique path. You can have a say in your life; you can escape the expectations that you learned from your school, work, family, and friends. No matter what you were told, you can start your life on a brand new slate. Yes, you can.

On December 26, 2004, a tsunami killed 30,957 men, women, and children in Sri Lanka. Many lives had fallen into a million little pieces. I flew to Sri Lanka to do aid work in my homeland where I had lived the first twenty years of my life. Along the coastal areas there was rubble scattered everywhere. Sights of chaos and despair were rampant. The colossal damage that the tidal waves had caused was incomprehensible. However, amidst that debris were a few women walking through the rubble and picking up broken bricks, one at a time. They were using the broken bricks to build new homes for themselves.

It was an inspiring sight. Here were women who had lost their children, husbands, friends, homes, communities, and everything else that came in between. Even that could not keep their spirits down. They found a way to pick up the broken pieces and build new lives for themselves. A few of them had made a conscious decision to steer their lives in a brand new direction, leaving their old lives behind. They had to; they had no other choice.

Sometimes, the only way to move forward with our lives is to come to terms with our ruined past and start anew, just like the tsunami victims of Sri Lanka did. Many people have a natural aptitude for learning new things; few, however, have the tenacity to leave yesterday behind and make new beginnings. Many of us have dreams, hopes, and aspirations, but it is our unwillingness to let go of our past that crushes our spirit most of the time.

Cleaning up your energy drains is a critical part of leaving yesterday behind. Some of the people closest to you may be energy drains, meaning they have no place in your creative life. Find new individuals who can provide you with meaning and fulfillment. Cleaning out can be hard, but worth it. If you want different results, you have to shuffle things around and start steering your life differently.

Now is the time to leave yesterday behind. Go out there and make a difference. Decide what is most important to you; whether it is to be a good wife, a dutiful mother, a career-oriented woman, a social worker, an entrepreneur, a spiritual healer, a loyal daughter, a supermom, or a combination of any of these. Whatever you do, give it two hundred percent.

Discover that greatness within you. You deserve it. You are great and you can become greater, if you want to. No one can make you feel less than beautiful — unless you let them.

Remind yourself of your beauty on a daily basis. Start each morning with three words that will transform your life for the better. Say "I am beautiful." Shine and make a difference. Take responsibility for your life and climb until your dreams come true.

Winding Roads of Success

GPS for Success

*I*magine how life would be if each one of us had a Global Positioning System planted within us.... This instrument, known as the GPS, would allow us to punch in directions of where we want to go in life and tell us exactly how to get there; with minimal errors and roadblocks of course. Some of the directions that we would plug into the GPS might look like this:

- · To become a millionaire by age thirty
- · To become the world's first trillionaire
- · To win a Nobel Prize
- · To become a loving mother
- · To become the fastest athlete
- · To be out of debt...
- · To leave our dark past behind and start over
  and more...

Well, guess what! We all have a built-in GPS within us. Only a few of us, however, have the knowledge to access it. Those who access that built-in GPS are the successful ones, overcoming obstacles and achieving their dreams without ever giving up.

None of the women in this book were born any more special than you or me. In fact, they probably had more shackles crippling them than most of us ever have. Yet, they tapped into their GPS to arrive at their destinations successfully. Their formula for success was a combination of several universal factors. Follow their directions and you, too, can achieve their level of greatness no matter where you are in life today.

Have you ever wondered why some people seem to achieve success effortlessly while others work just as hard but still remain unsuccessful? Here is why: Their GPS for success has been wired with a combination of character traits. Successful people think and act differently. Learn the twenty-four different ways that successful people think and act. If you, too, decide to follow their patterns of thinking and acting, success will come your way immediately.

1. Having a Dream

Dreams give us a reason for living. Without desires and dreams, the flame in our furnace dies out and life becomes mediocre, inspiration fades, depression sets in, and we stop creating and achieving. Dreaming brings us deep into the realm of well being and happiness, a place where we can design our life exactly as we would like it to be and tap into our creative spirit. The imagining can take any form: great relationships, a fulfilling career, a creative outlet, an enriching family experience, financial freedom, or being the queen at whatever we pursue. Only a few of us, however, are willing to do the work it takes to achieve our dreams.

> *"All our dreams can come true, if we have the courage to pursue them."*
>
> ~ Walt Disney

Every great dream begins with a dreamer. Always remember that you have within you the strength, the potential, and the passion to reach for the stars to change the world.

> *"So many of our dreams at first seem impossible, then they seem improbable, and then, when we summon the will, they soon become inevitable."*
>
> ~ Christopher Reeves

Reaching for your dreams enhances the meaning of your life. Once you launch your ideas into action, you feel better about yourself. Launching ideas to make your dreams come true is almost a prescription for boosting self esteem and happiness. People who achieve their dreams are happier and have higher self esteem.

Never underestimate the power of dreams and the influence of the human spirit. The potential for greatness lives within each of us. Each and every one of you can achieve greatness, if we seek it and make the necessary choices to make those dreams come true.

> *"The future belongs to those who believe in the beauty of their dreams."*
>
> ~ Eleanor Roosevelt

2. Taking Responsibility

Dreams and responsibility are two sides of the same coin. If you take responsibility for yourself, you will develop stamina to accomplish your dreams. Successful people seldom avoid responsibility from their lives. Rather, they embrace it. The "17 Women Who Shook the World" allowed no one and nothing to block their dreams, goals, and aspirations. They did not waste their time blaming others for their misery. Instead, they took responsibility for whatever happened to them and found realistic solutions.

"In dreams begins responsibility."

— William Butler Yeats

3. Problem Solving Attitude

There are two kinds of stones, one of which rolls. Similarly, there are two kinds of people on earth: problem seekers and problem solvers. Problem seekers are stagnant, whereas problem solvers are perpetually in motion. Problem seekers are constantly negative and complaining about the lack of a situation. That is their signature trait. Their goal is *not* to solve a problem and move on to enjoying life's riches. Rather, as soon as one problem has been taken care of, they are busy concocting another. Problem creation becomes an obsession. They spend a great deal of energy blaming others for their problems and rather than solving problems...they dwell on them.

Successful people, on the other hand, are problem solvers. They are attracted to solutions and untangling the knots in their lives. Successful people are capable of accomplishing tasks that seem impossible because they believe in solutions. Problem solvers are constantly in flowing motion, getting things done and moving on to achieving something new.

"It's not that I'm so smart, it's just that I stay with problems longer."

— Albert Einstein

Successful people understand that problems are opportunities to better things. They also see them as stepping stones to greater experiences rather than stumbling blocks to a stagnant state. When one door closes, another always opens.

Life is ten percent what happens to us and ninety percent how we respond to it. Different individuals act differently to the same circumstances. Unsuccessful people will *react* to problems while successful people tend to *respond* to them.

When problems come your way, embrace them, tackle them, and grow from them. Problems are only opportunities with a few thorns on them. Cultivate different tools to tackle a myriad of problems in effective ways. This allows you to address any problem that life throws at you.

"If you only have a hammer, you tend to see every problem as a nail."

—Abraham Maslow

4. Stop Feeling Like a Victim

Successful people are solution oriented rather than problem oriented. Typically, being problem oriented is a stance for feeling like a victim. When you call yourself a victim, you are seeking something from a situation. Victims are constantly in need of attention. Everything has to be about them, from the dinner table conversation over Thanksgiving to the family inheritance.

There are no "successful victims." You can either be successful or be a victim, but you cannot be both.

When there is a problem, successful people take a realistic approach to it and acknowledge its existence, rather than claiming a victim stance. They take action to tackle the problem rather than dwelling upon it or hiding it under the rug. Their goal is to take care of the problem as swiftly as possible in order to move on to something else. Successful people are constantly evolving and taking their lives to a different level.

"You don't drown by falling in the water; you drown by staying there."

— Edwin Louis Cole

5. Success is a Planned Goal

Successful people understand that success requires a process. They are continually evolving. They have big dreams, clear intentions, and are willing to go down any and every path to achieve their highest goals. They understand that seeking success and seeking popularity may not necessarily go hand-in-hand. Your own resolution to succeed is more important than anything else. Don't be fooled by anyone who says that success was an accident and not a planned goal. Belief in oneself is one of the most important bricks in building any successful venture.

Nearly all of the women featured throughout this book followed a formula for becoming successful. Achieving their goals was not a hit or miss type of endeavor. None of these women waited around like couch potatoes, waiting for success to knock on their doors. They planned their lives and lived their plans.

"Be the first to the field and the last to the couch."

— Proverb

6. Saying "Yes" to Life

Successful people trust their intuition. Rather than being subservient to societal conventions, adhering to limitations, or letting obstacles get in their way, they imagine themselves reaching the highest pinnacle. They are willing to take the leap and close all other doors that will keep them from achieving their dreams. They say "yes" to life rather than dwelling on "no."

"Never allow a person to tell you no who doesn't have the power to say yes."

— Eleanor Roosevelt

Truly successful people have fun with what they are doing and they are constantly in the flow of things. Sure, they work hard and have tension headaches, but they are doing something that they love, so that the hard work actually becomes pleasurable. The right people and situations are drawn to them. Their enthusiasm is contagious. They embrace affirmations on a daily basis.

*"After the final no there comes a yes
and on that yes the future of the world hangs."*

— Wallace Stevens

7. Taking Calculated Risks

Successful people are risk takers. They know that they cannot discover new oceans unless they have the courage to lose sight of the shore. A person who risks nothing does nothing, has nothing, is nothing, and becomes nothing. She simply cannot change and grow. Often the difference between a successful person and a failure is not that one has better abilities or ideas, but the courage that one has to take a calculated risk and to act. Successful people are resourceful and know that wherever they land, they will bounce back. They are ready to venture on paths untraveled. Risk-taking not only helps you to grow, but also can open up a new world.

*"Be not afraid of growing slowly. Be afraid
only of standing still."*

— Proverb

Do not fear risk. You have to trust the bridge to get to the other side of the river. Without challenge, you cannot reach the next level.

8. Unstoppable Attitude

Successful people are unstoppable when they truly want something. The more they take a chance, the more they leap. The more often they say "yes" or take risks that give them goose bumps, the more they will experience their creativity and intuition at work. They see the positive possibilities. Their unstoppable attitude allows them to direct the substantial energy of their frustration and turn it into positive, effective determination.

"Nothing can stop the man with the right mental attitude. Nothing on earth can help the man with the wrong mental attitude."

—Thomas Jefferson

9. Seeing Opportunities Where Others Find Problems

Successful people understand that there is little difference between obstacle and opportunity and are able to turn both to their advantage. Successful people see opportunities where others find frustration and problems. Successful people don't wait for opportunities to come. They get up and make them.

"A pessimist sees the difficulty in every opportunity; an optimist sees the opportunity in every difficulty."

—Winston Churchill

In a state of loss, creativity is down, the senses get numb, and there is lack of motivation and energy. It is a contagious energy that is passed on to others. An attitude of opportunity, on the other hand, breeds a higher energy level. It moves things from hopeless to fruitful. Opportunity often comes disguised in the form of misfortune or temporary defeat. Those on a quest for success always search for change, respond to it, and exploit it as an opportunity.

"No great man ever complains of want of opportunity."

— Ralph Waldo Emerson

10. Foregoing Advantages

Sometimes the best investments are the ones we don't make. It pays to decline advantages that can become encumbrances later on. Free lunches can cripple you from seeking opportunities. Successful people think carefully about situations that are too good to be true. They prefer to be independent and not feel under obligation to anyone as a result of accepting advantages in their quest for success.

"Next to knowing when to seize an opportunity, the most important thing in life is to know when to forego an advantage."

— Benjamin Disraeli

11. Believing in Yourself

Despite being belittled, laughed at, and humiliated, successful people always have a deep internal power propelling them forward.

Be yourself and have confidence in yourself. Start being fully who you are, even under the pressure, disdain, or misery of your current situation. Correct what doesn't work. No one and nothing allows you to do or not do something. In the end, it is you who is holding yourself back. Telling the truth about who you are and what you want will get the ball rolling to believing in yourself.

12. Embracing Life

Take pride in yourself and don't be afraid to say it. Allow no one to make you feel unworthy of living. No one has the permission to make you feel worthless except yourself. Start each day with these three simple words "I am beautiful," and never turn your back on life.

13. Find the Right Environment to Thrive

Plant your seeds in fertile territory where the likelihood of a bountiful harvest is high. Successful people find the right environment to thrive. They seek the environment where they would become most useful and productive.

Successful people are attracted to situations that demand more rather than less from them. They rarely dodge responsibility, danger, and hard work. Rather they are the bees. Work becomes their honey.

14. Step out of your Comfort Zone

Discomfort = growth. When you are being stretched beyond your comfort zone, you are being asked to grow. You have to take risks and be willing to be wrong. This is necessary to change your life for the better. If you remain in your comfort zone, you will not go any further.

The best and most productive moments in our lives typically occur when our body or mind is stretched to its limits to accomplish something very painful, difficult, and worthwhile.

"A ship in a harbor is safe, but that's not what a ship is built for. "

—Proverb

15. Living Life to the Fullest

Successful people spend each day as if it were their last. From the time they wake up until they go to bed, they are in a state of productivity. Gossip, idle talk, and wasting time are not a part of their routine. Life is limited. Time is limited. The choice to live life fully, however, is unlimited.

16. Allowing Others to do the Talking

Successful people rarely brag about their achievements or toot their own horns. They are unusually humble about their success, so they simply allow others to do the talking for them. They don't have time to talk about their greatness; nor is there the need. Their greatness is transparent and their substance keeps them silent.

" 'Tis the empty can that makes more noise. "

— Proverb

17. Taking Action

Successful people take action. Too often, we put off starting something because it seems far-fetched or seems to take too much energy. Some of us don't know how to follow through an idea or fear that it might change our lives too much. The reality is that when you have a map of how to get somewhere, it immediately seems much more attainable.

The only way to move forward is by taking a step. It can be a big step or a little step, and you usually have a choice of directions, but it is an action with a purpose behind it and no one else can do it for you. Occasionally, we slip backwards or make choices that undo some of our progress. The best step, however, that will cement your productive and possible beliefs is your own action. Take action today.

18. Believing in Now

Successful people know that if they want to be successful tomorrow then they need to think about the bottom line today. The power of now is important for them. Taking care of your now while you prepare for your new future is very important. Getting things in order makes you feel better immediately. Taking care of these today, rather than postponing them for tomorrow, gives you more power to influence your circumstances.

"Dig the well before you are thirsty."

—Proverb

19. Ignoring the Mind Chatter

Think of your mind as a large wicker basket. You can fill it up with nutritious fruit, fertile seeds, colorful vegetables, and a pot of fresh water, or you can fill it up with rotten eggs, stale milk, and dried up seeds. Great people know their mind chatter won't stop, so they don't waste their effort trying to control it. Instead, they take purposeful action that moves them toward manifesting their goals.

Rather than spending energy trying to change the course of the waters in the rivers of their minds, successful people observe them and learn how best to navigate them. This is what distinguishes the great from the near great. Successful people realize that either they dance with their goals or dance with their mind chatter. Goals will get them somewhere, mind chatter gets them nowhere.

20. Celebrating the Creative Process

Successful people are constantly being creative. They try different things, embracing what works and dumping the things that don't. They enjoy and celebrate the creative process. Creativity is an important part of becoming successful in life. Without an outlet for creativity, the human will is frustrated, depressed, and may engage in addictive behaviors.

The expression of creativity, either through a hobby, home, family, or career, is what leads us to fulfillment. If you are a housewife who has been baking country bread only for the past fifteen years, why not get creative and try kneading a focaccia for a change? If you have been in social work for the past thirty years and would like a career change as a ski instructor, why not seek it? Creativity can and should infiltrate every area of our lives: from meal preparation, shopping, writing, gifting, leadership, decorating, and vacationing to investment banking, marriage choices, and dressing for success.

21. Pariah to Piranha

Most people of achievement have been considered pariahs at some point. They were considered the outcastes, the unwanted, and in some cases, the "untouchables." People who have achieved any level of success in their lives rose from that to become the Piranha, the one to watch, and in some cases, the one to dread.

Successful people refuse to allow others to crush their spirits. When others throw stones at them, they pick them right up and build firm foundations. Standing firmly on those foundations, they use them as stepping-stones to propel themselves forward.

22. Stoic Resilience to Rejection

A stoic resilience to rejection is a key to becoming successful in whatever you set out to do in your life. Successful people don't give up on their ideas or on themselves. There is always the possibility of aiming higher and giving up eliminates all of that.

23. Strength of Mind

To succeed is to discipline a strong strength of mind. Successful people spend a good deal of time on meditation, intense concentration, and moving into a flowing state of mind. They learn to remove the clutter from their minds and fill them with ideas, plans, and actions that would allow them to achieve their goals. They do this on a daily basis.

"Where success is concerned, people are not measured in inches, or pounds, or college degrees, or family background; th ey are measured by the size of their thinking."

~ David Schwartz

24. Getting Off the Fence and Making Decisions

Your life begins to change when you make a conscious decision internally. Successful people realize that once they make one decision to make new beginnings, it is typically followed by a series of decisions that dot their entire lives. They have a clear sense of their priorities. Successful people have the ability to make decisions and stick to them. They don't sit on the fence and blame both sides for their indecisiveness.

Celebrating Success

Now that you have programmed these twenty-four steps into your internal GPS, success should be right around the corner. You might be wondering what happens when you've reached the pinnacle of success? Do you acknowledge it, celebrate, or just continue forward without any kind of jubilee?

There seems to be a myth that says if you celebrate or if you acknowledge the good in your life, somehow you will jinx yourself. The reality is the opposite. When you acknowledge what you have done, you are actually telling the universe that you are ready for more. Thus, if you recognize the good, you will get more good stuff. If you see the ugly, the problems, the lack of money, the hard work, and the stress, you will get more of that, too.

Anything done regularly becomes a habit. Celebrating, when done regularly, also becomes a habit. The more you can look for the good in your life, the more good you can see and the more your mind becomes programmed to celebrate it. Celebrating in any form is a way of positive acknowledgment.

Think Big to Become Successful

*S*uccessful people have one trait in common: They think big. In order to think big, they seize new opportunities that open new horizons for them. They move beyond their comfort zone and venture into the unknown. They are constantly redirecting their lives and they are willing to swing far out of their comfort zones. As a result, anything becomes possible.

Successful people venture from failure to failure, without loss of enthusiasm. All along, there is one character trait that persists — the courage to think big. People who change the world have the ability to see something new and innovative. They have the vision to make it better. Leaders are not afraid to be different, and the fear of failure does not prevent them from trying to create a better world. Eleanor Roosevelt once said, "You must do the things you think you cannot do." It is this vision of an improved world that inspires others to join leaders in their efforts to make change.

If you want different things to happen in your life, then you have to think differently, too. Since you have to think in any case, you might as well think big.

Big thinking allows you to dream big dreams. No matter what your profession is, big thinking can help to broaden your horizons and dream bigger dreams. If you embrace big thinking, your dreams will go from molehill to mountain size, and because you believe in possibilities, you will put yourself in the right position to achieve them.

What you think determines what you are willing to do. Lots of things are possible if you stop believing in your limits and you start thinking big. You have to make it possible in your head. Not probable, but possible, at least mentally. Big thinkers first insert the productive belief fully on their radar screen and then start behaving differently because of it. They understand that they can't improve and still stay the same.

It takes dedication and patience to think big. People who change the world understand that change does not nor will it happen overnight. Changing the world is an ongoing process.

"One never notices what has been done; one can only see what remains to be done."

— Marie Curie

It takes courage to think big. Courage means more than just saying what needs to be changed. It means deciding to be active in the effort to bring about change, no matter what it takes. Big thinkers face numerous challenges: they are criticized, made fun of, ignored, alienated from their friends and family, imprisoned, or even killed. They still embrace the courage to achieve larger things.

Big thinkers start with the premise that anything is possible and start with "I can." When you believe you can do something difficult, and you succeed, many doors open for you. If you want to achieve big things, you need to become a possibility thinker. Possibility thinking draws opportunities for you and for others. Possibility thinking also increases possibilities. You can't help but become more confident and think bigger when you are around possibility thinkers.

Big thinkers are genuinely happy for the success of others. They are not threatened by it. Feel the difference the minute you latch on to small thinkers — they are insecure, jealous of your success, and they will try to bring you down.

Thinking big can help you to live with wholeness and to live a very fulfilling life. People who see the big picture expand their experience because they expand their world. The lens through which they view the world is constantly in a state of flux and never stagnant.

Big picture thinkers are continuously learning and listening to others. They know that by listening, rather than talking, they can learn. They are always visiting new places, reading new books, meeting new people, learning new skills, and exploring new projects. They realize that there is a world out there besides their own. They make an effort to get outside of themselves and see other people. They see things from the other person's point of view. Big picture thinkers are usually more tolerant of other people and their thinking.

To get things done successfully, you need focus. Big thinkers create paintings of where they want to be. They envision success beforehand and then work towards it. It is like an architect drawing a blueprint first, and then contractors working around that plan. However, to get the right things done, you also need to consider the big picture. Big picture thinking keeps you on target and helps to stay in focus.

Teamwork is an important part of thinking big. For a team project to be successful, it is important that team members see the whole picture and not just their own part. The better the grasp team members have of the big picture, the greater their potential is to work together.

Big picture thinkers remove small thinking. They don't get caught up in the mundane like small thinkers do. Manipulative behaviors, gossiping, and small talk are not a part of their vocabulary. Big thinkers are like rolling stones; they don't gather moss. Big thinkers invest themselves in what they believe can succeed, that can bring some sort of productive result.

Big thinkers value time. Time is precious because it is limited. Life is a short journey with an overwhelming "to-do" list for big thinkers. Every second counts.

People who think big broaden their outlook by striving to learn from every experience. They are not afraid of failing. Failure makes them stronger and motivates them to succeed. Their biggest teachers are their mistakes. They learn from both positive and negative experiences. People who think big know that their roads are filled with uncertainties and struggles. They embrace uncertainty with self confidence, rather than avoiding it. They embrace difficulties rather than running away from them. They try a lot of different things, take a lot of chances, and take time to learn after every victory or defeat.

People who think big understand that some of their past behavioral patterns and ways of thinking may be harmful to their progress. They are willing to let go of being right all the time. Big thinkers would rather be successful than be right. They are willing to admit their mistakes and learn from others.

Thinking big is infectious. Success is contagious. When one person takes a big leap and goes for it, others around her are inspired to do the same, most of the time.

A direct correlation exists between big thinking and the level of a person's energy. Big thinking gives you more energy. When you embrace big thinking, you believe in what you are doing and that gives you energy.

How many highly successful people do you know who are continually negative? None. How many impossibility thinkers are you acquainted with who achieve big things? None. People with a "it-can't-be-done" mind-set have two choices: they can expect, and continually experience, the worst or they can change their thinking. If you think you can, then you can. If you think you can't, then you can't. Big thinking eliminates attracting naysayers into your life. Inviting negative people into your life is a sure way to steer you off your track and darken your path to success.

Big thinkers dream one size bigger. One of the best ways to cultivate a possibility mind-set is to prompt yourself to dream one size bigger than you normally do. Most people dream too small. If you push yourself to dream more expansively, to imagine yourself one size bigger, to make your goals at least a step beyond what makes you comfortable, you will be forced to grow.

Sometimes, our circumstances may deter us from thinking big. An oppressive marriage, abusive parents, cruel siblings, oppressive political governments that crush creative thinking, financial shackles, and ill health may make it difficult to think big. None of these shackles, however, can remove hope. There is always hope for a better tomorrow. Most of the time, however, the only thing stopping us from thinking big is ourselves, not our family, not the society that we live in, and not our religious beliefs. We sabotage our own success.

Dream and give yourself permission to envision a You that you choose to be. Yes, you ARE big.

Winding Journeys and Less Traveled Roads

*T*he United States has had a long and winding journey in her "Women's Rights Department." Many women sacrificed their lives in order to fight for their freedom while other women throughout history have been ostracized for fighting for women's rights.

Native American Women

In many Native American cultures men waged war, hunted, and governed, while women and girls planted, cultivated, and harvested crops. They made pottery and baskets, tanned hides for clothing, dried and prepared food, and constructed housing. In some Native American tribes, women held high positions. Women were sometimes chiefs. They served as healers and spiritual leaders, called shamans.

Women in the 1600s

In 1565, the Spanish established St. Augustine in Florida, the first permanent European colony in North America. In the American colonies in the 1600s, being born a girl or boy was the most important factor in a person's life. It determined the way she or he was raised. Girls learned to cook, garden, preserve food, milk cows, make butter, care for younger children, and a hundred other tasks. If their hands were not needed at home, then, older girls worked as maids in homes where help was needed. Women also traded. They bartered or sold cheese, butter, pies, knits, and poultry. Women had total responsibility for the home. They worked from sun up to sun down and beyond.

Most colonists who settled in the "New World," brought the belief with them that women were weak in character and mind. Because women were considered weak, there were many things they were not allowed to do. They were forbidden to speak in both church and government. They could not vote or hold office. Women had few rights before the law. If a woman broke the rules and spoke up publicly, she could be taken to court.

Wives had to obey their husbands. Women were sometimes fined or publicly whipped for disobeying too openly. It was a wife's duty to raise the child according to her husband's instructions. Although divorce was rare, it was more common in New England than in the middle and southern colonies, because the Puritans considered marriage a civil agreement rather than a religious commitment. When divorce did occur, the children belonged to the husband.

The Quakers who began settling in New England after 1650 considered men and women equal before God. Quaker women were allowed to speak and preach. Some Quaker women grew up to be independent and free thinkers.

Women in the 1700s

By 1700, the population in North America was estimated at about one million, with more than 10,000 Africans and about 350,000 Europeans among them. During this time period, almost everything that families needed was still produced at home, much of it by women. Wherever they were, girls were busy. Most women did not have the money to hire anyone to help. For them maintaining a home was exhausting. Most women who stayed at home cooked large meals every day and baked. They boiled and rinsed the wash one day each week and ironed the next. In the summer they canned.

Some women relied entirely on money that they earned themselves. This was especially true for widows and unmarried women without families. Almost all the young women in the colonies married, sometimes because marriage was the best way for them to make a living.

During slavery times, Black people had their own doctors who prescribed cures often unknown to Whites. Because they believed more in roots and herbs than in treatments favored at the time, which included purging, bleeding, and blistering, their healer was called the "Root Doctor."

Many male doctors believed all women were diseased and refused to examine them. The quieter and sicklier a woman was, the more attractive she became. A woman could not vote, serve on juries, or testify in court. No law stopped a husband or father from hitting a wife or daughter, though some laws spelled out how big an object could be used.

Childbearing was an important and dangerous time. Husbands were not typically present during deliveries. They stayed away until the blood was mopped up, the afterbirth buried, and the baby had sucked several meals. Some women were given whisky to ease labor pains.

Life was hard for everyone, but during the 1700s there was some relief for wealthier women. They could buy dairy products, poultry, and homespun cloth made in the colonies. The finer houses in towns were usually brick or clapboard and were more comfortable than the crude log or sod houses of the century before.

The opportunities for women to earn money widened. After 1750 a few merchants gathered women and girls into the first low-paying workshops. Women were still usually related to domestic work but there were many exceptions. Married women helped with family businesses and farms and managed them when their husbands were away.

Women During the American Revolution

During the American Revolution, from 1775-1783 when the thirteen colonies waged a war for independence from England, women worked even harder. With their husbands away, full responsibility for farms and businesses fell on them. Most women did not work outside the home, but they labored quite hard inside it. Even before the fighting broke out women led the boycott of British goods. Instead of purchasing cloth from England, women wove or bought "homespun," just as they had during the first one hundred and fifty years in the colonies. Women may have worked to make themselves and their families successful, but it was the men who got most of the credit. It was a sign of the times.

During the war, women's organizations raised money and made clothes for the troops. Women were also spies. Women broke new ground during the Revolutionary War by writing and talking about politics.

On July 4, 1776, John Adams and the other members of the Continental Congress in Philadelphia had declared the American colonies independent of England. "Remember the ladies," Abigail Adams wrote to her husband in 1776. "Do not put such unlimited power into the hands of the husbands." Abigail Adams represented a new trend among women. Before the American Revolution, few women questioned their place in society. After the Revolution, a married woman's property still belonged to her husband. Women could not yet vote or hold office. Their presence in public activities was either prohibited or loudly denounced.

However, the Revolution changed women's ideas about marriage. Many women who had operated family businesses or farms during the war began to think of marriage as a partnership and an economic contract. No longer did they believe that their husbands should make all the decisions. Also, more women wanted to choose their husbands rather than leave the selection to their parents. Yes, the American Revolution brought about some changes in women's lives.

Women in the Early 1800s

By 1801, 5.3 million people lived in the United States. America of the early 1800s laced itself up tight. Personal ambition in a woman was thought to be evil. Childbearing and housekeeping were her duties. No college was open to her. Respectable jobs were mostly dreary, and any wages paid to a married woman went straight to her husband. If she divorced, she could lose her children, property, and reputation.

Women had few opportunities. The occupations that yielded money to women were severely limited: teaching, midwifery, prostitution, and for the select few, writing. The fields of law, medicine, business, education, and politics excluded women. Breaking free from these standards was nearly impossible. Everything depended on finding a man to marry. Then, cooped and caged, married women had to do whatever their husbands wished them to do. Women's lives were an endless round of pregnancies, childbearing, and domestic duties. They worked hard and died young.

Jobs were still plentiful for men, and there was little in the way of respectable work for women. Domestic work was available, but that was most often taken by single immigrant women paid the equivalent of slave wages. Women worked in low-paying industrial occupations. The growth of industry and cities created more work for girls and women outside the home than ever before. Thousands moved from farms into cities to earn wages in water-powered textile mils. Others made shoes in factories.

Women in the Mid-1800s

Women were still the "weaker sex." A popular book of the day was titled *The Physiological Feeble Mindedness of Woman*. A good way to rid oneself of an independent minded wife was to confine her to an insane asylum. A French critic wrote that "a woman's place is simply for sex and to reproduce." The rare female intellectual was depicted as masculine, coarse, ugly, careworn, and industrious, but making no significant contribution.

Heaven help the woman who might aspire to becoming a doctor, lawyer, or an engineer. Though not altogether impossible to achieve such career goals, any woman setting her sights on them had to understand that the profession she had chosen was difficult to attain at best and if she was not endowed with an uncommon supply of fortitude, probably impossible.

Thousands of young women became teachers, often with little education themselves. Women insisted on better education. Girls' schools sprang up. Girls studied reading, writing, grammar, geography, public speaking, and arithmetic. Near the end of the century, women pounded typewriters and collected fares on streetcars. What marriage meant in 1853 was a woman's legal bondage to the man whose name she assumed, for better and, just as often, for worse. Her wealth and her children were his property. He had the right to reclaim her if she left him and, in most states, he had the right to beat her, provided he did so with a 'reasonable' instrument. If he prospered, she shared in his wealth, but if he were to drink or gamble away the family's money, she had a legal duty as his wife to follow him obediently into ruin. The law said that the husband and wife were one — and that "one" was the husband.

To marry a good provider and look after his household and children was just about all most conventional women dared hope for. If a woman had to work outside the home or simply chose to do so, the options were on the sparse and none too lucrative side. Maids were always in demand, of course, and it was possible to get various types of factory work deemed suitable for a woman.

Women in the Civil War

Between 1861-1865, the Civil War ended slavery. The War Between the States — United States of America (Union) and the new nation called the Confederate States of America or the Confederacy — started in April 1861. More than three million men fought. When the war started, there were fewer than 15,000 soldiers in the army. In order to fight a war, the federal government had to call for volunteers.

The government did not supply uniforms for any soldiers except those in the standing U.S. Army. Men in the civilian army had to find their own uniforms. Usually, they were stitched by women with a sewing machine powered by a foot treadle invented in 1849. The sewing machine provided employment in factories where women worked for fifteen to sixteen hours a day, for which the wage was $3 a week. The sewing machine revolutionized the garment industry. Women began sewing at home. Unmarried women who made their living by spinning were called "spinsters."

During the Civil War, women of both North and South found their lives and their hopes changed. They did much more in the war than defend their homes or wait for their soldiers to come home. They fought. They spied. They supplied the troops.

The role that American women played in taking care of the sick and wounded during the Civil War was astounding. As soon as the war started, women went out to the battlefields to care for the wounded. As deaths and losses mounted, accepting women as nurses seemed the only way to care for wounded and ill soldiers.

In July 1861, the Federal Government established the United States Sanitary Commission. This was done at the urging of such prominent women as Dr. Elizabeth Blackwell, the first woman in the United States to earn a medical degree. When women volunteers of the Sanitary Commission came into a hospital camp run by male doctors, the men usually resented their presence. The women carried on the work that needed doing without permission or help.

At least one woman is known to have served as a military physician during the Civil War — Mary Walker. When the war started, Mary was unable to get any army officials to take seriously her request to serve. She volunteered at tent hospitals, first in Virginia and then in Tennessee. Finally, in 1863, she was given an official appointment as an army doctor. When the war was over, she became the only woman to receive a Congressional Medal of Honor.

Some women disguised themselves as men and became true soldiers. More than four hundred women are known to have gone to war as actual soldiers. Most soldiers who were identified as women were discovered only after they were killed or wounded. Perhaps the longest serving woman was Jennie Hodgers of Illinois, who fought as "Albert Cashier" through the whole war and then lived as Cashier the rest of her life. She was not identified as a woman until she was injured in an automobile accident. She persuaded the doctor to keep her secret. In her old age, when asked why she joined the army, she replied, "The country needed men, and I wanted excitement."

Women often accompanied army regiments as a combination of nurse and mascot. They were called "vivandieres" or "daughters of the regiment."

After the men had left for the war, many women were left alone with children to support. Farm wives spent four rugged years doing the man's work of running the farm, the woman's work of feeding and raising the family, and the war work of spinning, weaving, knitting, and rolling bandages. The end of the war found many Southern women exhausted and often quite ill. Yet, they kept their own homes going and their children growing.

Most war-related activities and sacrifices of Southern women were of a private nature. Many women gave up meat and other foods that could be used as rations for soldiers. They often became ill with malnutrition. Some women who could do little else wrote letters every week to every soldier they knew, hoping that the letters would help to encourage and cheer the fighting men. Almost every woman within a hundred miles of a battle site was sent sick or wounded soldiers for her to nurse in her home.

Women made unimaginable sacrifices to help their male counterparts. As funds to continue the war were used up, women dug deeper and deeper into their own treasures to contribute to the cause. Their jewels became cash. They turned their carpets into soldiers' carpets and their everyday dresses into men's shirts.

During the previous decade, many women had fought for their rights, but now they tacitly agreed to postpone equality and enfranchisement for the war effort. Lucy Stone gave up the income from her women's rights lectures and made shirts for Union soldiers. Mary Livermore, a Chicago Women's Rights Advocate, began what was to become four years of visiting camps and hospitals, organizing sanitary aid societies, and meeting countless times with President Lincoln. Mary Livermore was also responsible for encouraging farmers into donating fresh fruit, which was then rushed by rail to the troops.

Women became creative. They invented substitutes for coffee, such as toasted seeds and burnt corn. They made shoes out of squirrel skin or braided straw. They dug up the ground under smokehouses, retrieved the salt used in preserving meat, and then used it again.

By April 1865, the United States was on the threshold of what promised to be a new beginning. Robert E. Lee surrendered to Ulysses S. Grant on April

9th, officially ending the Civil War. Lincoln's assassination on April 14, 1865, brought a moral void. The country suffered a pervasive sense of despair. There was no longer any point in playing by the rules.

Woman Suffrage Movement in the Early 1900s

New ideas on women's rights and economic and social equality were being espoused and experimented throughout the country. Women had been the backbone of the religious revival movement in the early part of the nineteenth century. Women had been encouraged to express their beliefs in public. They were invited to discuss subjects, most notably Abolition, that previously had been viewed as the domain of men.

The woman suffrage movement was among the largest, longest lived, and politically significant mass reform movements in U.S. history. It had an impact on the life of every American, regardless of race, nationality, creed, age, or gender. The woman suffrage movement demanded that the U.S. population consider the most fundamental issue of a democracy: who shall be entitled to enjoy all the rights and privileges of a democratic society and who shall be excluded. From the time that the first woman suffrage amendment was proposed in Congress in 1868 until the ratification of the 19th Amendment in 1920, more than fifty years of ceaseless agitation ensued.

During the early 1900s, almost half the people in the United States lived in cities and twenty percent of the paid workers were women. Women worked as nurses, teachers, typists, domestics, and sales clerks. Women with jobs worked hard. One factory owner said he hired women immigrants when he could because "they keep at it like horses."

In 1916, Jeanette Rankin of Montana became the first woman to be elected to the United States Congress. The United States fought in World War I, which began in Europe in 1914. In 1919, Congress finally proposed an amendment to the Constitution that would allow women to vote. By 1920, the 19th Amendment to the Constitution was passed, giving women right to vote in all elections.

The Civil Rights Movement in the 1960s

The American Civil Rights Movement refers to the period from 1954 to 1968 when many people joined together to try to end racial discrimination. Thousands of women were busy following the lead of nineteenth century activists who had pushed for women's suffrage. Many worked through the National American Woman Suffrage Association (NAWSA). During the 1960s, women became politically active. It was an explosive time in America. Women demanded equality. Women fought for the freedom to compete for any job. They wanted lives outside the home. The Civil Rights Movement gained broader support in the United States. In many states, African Americans still had to use separate waiting areas in doctors' offices and train stations. They even had to use separate water fountains. In addition, some African Americans were refused their voting rights through various methods. They had to take unfair tests before they could vote. In Montgomery, Alabama, an African American woman named Rosa Parks was arrested for not giving up her seat to a White man on a city bus.

Women of 2012 and Beyond

The life of a woman, today, is determined by three factors: the country she is born in, the family she is born into, and the time period of her birth. Every country is moving at its own pace when it comes to the advancement of women's rights. In some countries today, women still lead lives that they led five hundred years ago, while in others this has changed. Come 2015, women in Saudi Arabia will finally be able to vote and hold political office. This was a right that women in the United States started to enjoy in 1870, when Esther Morris became the first woman to hold political office in South Pass City, Wyoming. On the other hand, in 1965 Sri Lanka (formerly known as Ceylon) became the first country to produce a female head of government, something that the United States has yet to do.

Today, women can make more choices than ever. Some women have chosen to stay single while others refuse to live in unhappy marriages and seek independence. Some are "supermoms" who balance jobs, social service, and families. More and more women are fighting corruption, breaking down old prejudices, starting businesses, and entering fields like politics that, for centuries, were considered off limits for women.

The payoff for women's empowerment is priceless. It will result in a new world order that no one can ever imagine. At present, the world needs women's idealism and determination, perhaps more in politics than anywhere else. Women haven proven that, as leaders, their best is every bit as good as men's, and their worst is just as bad. Some women are born warriors. Their instinct for survival and taking care of their cubs in the den is ingrained. Women are good caregivers and make excellent providers.

We are going to see more female leaders emerging all over the world. There will soon be a day when female heads of state will outnumber males.

A Lady in the White House

History tried to erase her from the books, but failed. In 1872, Victoria Woodhull was the first woman in American history to seek the United States Presidency. In many people's eyes, men and women alike, running for president made her a monster. Among the mildest of the names they called Victoria Woodhull was "Mrs. Satan."

As they saw it, Victoria Woodhull rudely violated conventional ideas of what was proper behavior for her sex/gender. She also totally rejected the traditional view that a woman has no right to be ambitious or competitive. Whether as presidential nominee, radical feminist, stock broker, newspaper editor, socialist, public speaker, free lover, or divorcee, Victoria Woodhull gloried in her independence. They ridiculed her, put her in jail, and put up terrifying posters of her on the streets. Victoria knew that she was "ahead of her time." Some 140 years later, America has still failed to produce a female head of state. Is Victoria Woodhull still ahead of her time? Is America ready for a woman in the White House today?

In the late 1970s, when Congresswoman Pat Schroeder was asked how she could be both a mother and a congresswoman, she responded bluntly, "God gave me a brain and a uterus and I intend to use them both" (*Time*, 1978).

For centuries, political ambition has been considered "unwomanly." The barriers with attitudes to a female president stretch far back into Western history. Christianity itself has produced some of the most effective strictures against women being in public service with 1 Corinthians 14:34 telling us: "Let your women keep silence in the churches: for it is not permitted unto them to speak; but are not commanded to be under obedience as also saith the law" (King James Version).

American women were excluded not only from suffrage and other aspects of citizenship like jury service and military service, but also the rights of property and bodily integrity. Over time this has carved out a system that transfers a woman's civic identity to her husband with the institution of marriage. In lieu of civil status, early American women were subjected to the "Cult of True Womanhood." According to this standard, the virtuous woman was one untouched by both private vice and public life. Women were expected to remain behind the scenes. They were to be seen, not heard. Female virtue emphasized women taking a backseat and being pious and submissive to their male counterparts. Men took up paid positions in inner-city factories while women tended the home and raised children according to her husband's wishes. This created a tidy division between the private (female) sphere and the public (male) sphere.

Any woman entering the public realm tarnished her good name and invited social stigma. During Puritan times, it also meant possible excommunication. Against this backdrop, it is no wonder that American women for so long did not succeed in their suffrage quest, officially begun in 1848 with the Declaration of Sentiments at Seneca Falls, New York, and which continues to this day.

How is it that citizens of the United States who pride themselves on democratic principles and women's equality have never elected a woman as President? Beginning with Victoria Woodhull in 1872, the following lists some of the women who have run for the office of the presidency as major party candidates:

NAME	YEAR	PARTY
Victoria Woodhull	1872	Equal Rights
Belva Lockwood	1884, 1888	Equal Rights
Margaret Chase Smith	1964	Republican
Shirley Chisholm	1972	Democratic
Patsy Takamoto Mink	1972	Democratic
Ellen McCormack	1976	Democratic
Patricia Schroeder	1988	Democratic
Elizabeth Dole	2000	Republican
Carol Moseley Braun	2004	Democratic
Hillary Rodham Clinton	2008	Democratic

In recent decades, there have been four predictable paths to the White House that seem to provide presidential hopefuls with the credentials and resources necessary for a successful campaign. These four paths are: military, the vice presidency, governorship, and Congress.

The job title of "President of the United States," or "Commander-in-Chief," demands a warrior spirit and is infused with the notion of the "citizen soldier." Military service is recommended as a "prerequisite" to the Commander-in-Chief position. This can become a difficult task for women, who are thought to be more experienced in domestic policy areas like education and health care. Military service is atypical for women to excel.

Though notions of womanhood have in some ways changed dramatically in the intervening decades, any woman running for the White House today is still running with hundreds of years of ideological baggage strapped to her ankles. It is no wonder that female candidates come under intense scrutiny and humiliation.

A woman trying to fulfill a masculine role is not fondly looked at by society. Some expect a dainty and soft role to be played by women. The same goes for a man. A man doing "unmanly" things may have a hard time making it to the White House. A man performing feminine duties can be appalling to some parts of society. Similarly, a woman performing masculine roles seems to be looked down upon. Each gender is expected to present a display of a certain type of behavior, and yet, this sometimes goes against their gender.

The notion of being the "first" woman to become president often becomes a way of treating the female candidate as an interesting novelty rather than a serious contender. It implies a lack of experience. A woman running for president may need to devise a gender strategy that carefully avoids overt displays of femininity or drawing attention to her sex. Female candidates are expected to lean toward the masculine rather than the feminine. Some, however, find this gender "crossing" rather troubling.

The emphasis in news coverage of Senate campaigns on largely male issues like foreign policy and the economy than "female" issues like health care and education also tend to go against women. Women are seen as caregivers in most societies. They are seen as being soft and mild, rather than rough and aggressive. By the same token, a woman acting too aggressively is frowned upon by many. Since the public tends to associate women with inherent capabilities regarding "care" issues, this focus on "male" issues can further disadvantage women candidates.

References are made to female candidates' physical attributes. The designer clothes she wears, how she styles her hair, the colors she wears, and the styling of clothes seem to play an important part on the part of media scrutiny. It is less typical to hear the discussion of the type of gel a male candidate uses or how he combs his hair at political gatherings.

Personality is also a focus of media coverage. Media coverage of elections tends to focus heavily on the candidates' characters, but this pattern appears to be heightened for women. For example, is she married or unmarried? Does she have children or is she childless? These are the types of questions that sometimes arise with female presidential candidates.

Female candidates are warned of showing much emotion in public, since doing so presumably will generate media coverage that plays into public stereotype of female emotions. The displaying of emotions on the part of female candidates is also seen as a sign of weakness.

Most voters can only encounter presidential candidates via the mass media. Thus, the media's persistent emphasis on a candidate's negativity and their down-playing of the substantive attributes of female candidates in particular, may mask voters' understandings of the candidates and the issues at stake in any election while fundamentally disadvantaging female contenders. The media may shift its emphasis to a female candidate's looks rather than the policies she stands for. Mainstream media coverage is one of the few avenues by which presidential candidates can reach mass audience aside from television advertising.

As of 2012, only two women have been nominated for vice president of a major party: Geraldine Ferraro in 1984 and Sarah Palin in 2008. Yet, no woman has yet been vice president either. In 2008, Senator Hillary Rodham Clinton came closer than any woman in history to the U.S. presidency. For those citizens concerned with the status of women in the United States, the 2008 election proved many things: that women can be viable national candidates, that they can overcome at least some gender barriers in media coverage, and that they can assume different gender strategies. Yes, the year 2008 became a milestone in the transformation of gender politics.

Thus, a woman has never made it to the White House — yet. Many have attempted it since Victoria Woodhull did in 1872, but so far everyone has failed with many being ridiculed for even entertaining the thought. Shirley Chisholm ran in 1972, saying, "I ran for President because most people think the country is not ready for a black candidate, not ready for a woman candidate. Someday…"

It is time for a female president in the United States of America...

Success Stories of
17 Amazing Women

Susan B. Anthony

A Lifetime of Devotion to Women's Causes

Susan B. Anthony immersed her life in the women's suffrage movement.

· Born in 1820

· Fought to improve the status of women

· Active Abolitionist

· Got women the right to vote and to run for political office

· Her motto was: "No man is good enough to govern any woman without her consent."

· Died in 1906

For the first half of Susan B. Anthony's life, thousands of African American women worked as slaves. They were treated as nothing more than property, with few rights and almost no personal freedom. Anthony fought hard to change that. Perhaps the most heartening part of her legacy is her conviction that all one needs to overcome an obstacle is boundless determination and more hard work. By the time slavery was abolished in the mid 1860s, Anthony had found her calling; improving the status of all American women. Today, her very name is a symbol of women's struggle for the right to vote and run for public office.

Birth and Quaker Background

Susan Brownell Anthony was born in Adams, Massachusetts, on February 15, 1820. In 1833, the Anthony family moved to New York. In general, girls of the early nineteenth century attended school for only a few years and were instructed in only the most basic skills, which were reading, writing, and simple arithmetic. They were deprived of the opportunity to study mathematics, the sciences, Latin, and Greek, which were considered essential to a boy's education.

Susan's father resolved that he must provide an exemplary education for all his children regardless of gender, a very unusual decision for middle class parents in the 1830s, but Daniel Anthony wanted much more for his daughters.

He ensured that his daughters received the same quality education that sons would receive. Unhappy with the education in the area, her father established a school for his children and for the children of his neighbors who were willing to contribute to the teacher's salary. A special schoolroom was set aside for the "home-school" in their own home. Daniel Anthony employed only the most highly educated women for his school.

The Anthony family was a Quaker family. By the time Susan B. Anthony was born, Quakers had been living in the United States for more than 150 years. English Quakers first settled in the colonies suffering intense persecution in the American colonies. The Quakers differed from other Protestant denominations. Quakers believe that all people have the ability and potential to understand and communicate the word of God.

Daniel Anthony was noted for his antislavery views. His home was a meeting place for a wide variety of people interested in social reform, and Susan B. Anthony took advantage of the opportunity to learn as much as possible. Susan B. Anthony's parents played a critical role in forming her as an individual who thought for herself and did what she believed was right, rather than following the herd. Unlike many of her female Abolitionists, Anthony had the devoted support of her parents and siblings throughout her career in reform.

Unlike many other female Abolitionists, Susan B. Anthony (right) had the devoted support of her family throughout her career in reform.

Daniel Anthony wanted his children to attend Quaker meetings. As Quakers, the Anthony children were not allowed to sing or dance. The Quakers were also unique because they permitted women to participate in church affairs, such as to speak at Quaker meetings, to pursue the ministry, and to voice their opinions about church government. Since the Quaker view maintained that the Inner Light resided within each person regardless of gender, they did not strictly interpret biblical scriptures that restricted or forbade women's public activity as most Protestant sects did. Anthony's parents encouraged Susan's natural sense of independence, a trait that would shape the rest of her life. Because of her Quaker upbringing, Anthony grew up never questioning her rights to voice her opinion or her equal opportunity to assume an active role in society.

Teaching Career

At her father's direction, Susan B. Anthony began her career as a teacher in her father's home school during the summer. She was fifteen years old. Later, she taught at the local district school. Daniel Anthony was criticized by other middle class adults of their community who believed that it was improper for a man of his social standing to allow his daughters to work outside the home and earn money. Nevertheless, Daniel Anthony was wholeheartedly committed to ensuring that all his children possessed the skills to be self-sufficient, independent adults.

Soon, Susan B. Anthony became an independent woman, becoming the headmistress of an all-girl school. For the first time she got to spend the money that she earned on herself. She liked that financial independence. Her parents also allowed her the freedom to follow her own path without making demands that she marry, visit them frequently, support the family financially, or help with their household affairs. This was also unusual for parents of daughters during the nineteenth century, as daughters were expected to fulfill such duties. Thus, Susan B. Anthony had an atypical upbringing, unfettered by societal norms and family demands. Hers was an example of her family giving the fullest support in the path she chose to pursue. This lifted many barriers for her personally and created shortcuts for her to achieve her career goals.

Political Activism Work

Susan B. Anthony had not been teaching long when she discovered that women teachers received a fraction of a male teacher's salary, even though women taught just as many students and worked as hard and as many hours as men. She resented the saying, "Join the union, girls, and together say Equal Pay for Equal Work."

"I don't want to die as long as I can work; the minute I cannot, I want to go."

The 1850s were years of incessant activism for Anthony. Her friendships with Elizabeth Cady Stanton, Lucy Stone, and Antoinette Brown were extremely important. Her associations with these women taught her about the world of reform, feminism, and the art of oratory.

When the 14th Amendment to the Constitution was ratified in 1868, it guaranteed the vote to all male citizens at least twenty-one years of age. Anthony protested the restriction, arguing that women were citizens and should be able to vote.

As the "Napoleon" of the women's rights movement, Anthony believed that her primary task was to educate society about the crucial importance of the ballot for all citizens in a democracy. "There can be but one possible way for women to be freed from the degradation of disenfranchisement and that is through the slow process of agitation and education, until the vast majority of women themselves desire freedom," she once said.

"I have encountered riotous mobs and have been hung in effigy, but my motto is: Men's rights are nothing more. Women's rights are nothing less."

Assembling a small group of like-minded acquaintances, Anthony formed the "Woman's State Temperance Society of New York." Anthony took her campaign across the state and then around the country. She spoke out for a woman's right to own property, to maintain custody of children after divorce, and to vote in state and national elections.

In 1869, Wyoming had given women the right to vote in territorial elections — the year Susan B. Anthony helped establish the National Suffrage Association. Many people laughed at her ideas, but in 1872 Anthony managed to register and cast a vote in Rochester. She was arrested, tried, and fined. However, this did not stop her from going head-on and immersing in women's rights.

Susan B. Anthony educated women and men alike through her sweeping cross-country lecture tours, her responsiveness to members of the press, and her extensive lobbying of state legislators and members of Congress, as well as through petition drives, speeches at congressional hearings, state suffrage campaigns, and the dialogue she cultivated with scores of national and state suffragists. She especially looked forward to the day when women would share government with men. In each suffrage speech, Anthony made sure that her audience comprehended the disgrace and humiliation of disenfranchisement. She argued that convicted criminals and the mentally incompetent were the only other individuals with whom women shared the degradation of political powerlessness. Anthony had the highest expectations for a world made perfect by women's votes.

Ideas on Marriage

Susan B. Anthony did not view marriage as an institution for a woman to become dependent on a man. This was progressive thinking and stirred many minds.

"I declare to you that a woman must not depend upon the protection of man, but must be taught to protect herself, and there I take my stand."

As she entered her thirties, Anthony felt that her chances of finding a man who would respect and uphold her reform career was negligible. By this time, she was solidly dedicated to her women's rights work and she accepted this career path for herself. While she never swore off marriage, her political activism consumed her. For the rest of her life, Anthony maintained her conviction that for women, marriage and a leadership role in reform were not compatible. Thus, social service became her sole purpose of life.

The quest for women's rights filled Anthony with a light so brilliant and a fire so unquenchable that no obstacle could compete with her near fanatical determination to blast open the doors of democracy. She always reinforced that women should be independent and believed there was nothing greater than independence. It was alright to be single.

"I think the girl who is able to earn her own living and pay her own way should be as happy as anybody on earth. The sense of independence and security is very sweet."

Abolitionist Movement

Although Susan B. Anthony is primarily remembered for her work in the women's rights and woman suffrage movements, she was a zealous Abolitionist, well-known for her years of uncompromising, passionate work to gain freedom for the slaves.

The American Anti-Slavery Society (AASS) was one of the primary national Abolitionist organizations in the United States. Much of the work and activity of the AASS was achieved through its auxiliary societies. These regional, state,

Although Susan B. Anthony is primarily remembered for her work in the women suffrage movements, she was a zealous Abolitionist.

and local organizations sponsored lectures and conventions to rally support for Abolitionism, published antislavery newspapers, and disseminated antislavery literature. The AASS organized fund-raising events and, in many areas, assisted local African Americans with education and housing.

Susan B. Anthony's involvement in the AASS, particularly her years as an antislavery agent (1856-1861) and her close working relationships with other AASS activists, was crucial to her development as an Abolitionist and as a women's rights and suffrage reformer.

For Anthony, a long-cherished dream of a career in Abolitionism was realized in 1856 when she was asked to be an agent for the state of New York. Anthony eagerly accepted and, for $10 a week, from 1856 through the winter of 1861, she organized antislavery lectures and meetings from Albany to Buffalo.

"The older I get, the greater power I seem to have to help the world. I am like a snowball: the further I am rolled, the more I gain."

Susan B. Anthony worked tirelessly. The older she got, the more work she felt was to be done. "Oh, if I could but live another century and see the fruition of all the work for women! There is so much yet to be done," she said.

Anthony died March 13, 1906, in Rochester. Fourteen years later, the 19th Amendment was passed, granting full suffrage to women. Many people called it the "Anthony Amendment."

The Strides She Made

Anthony was a powerful leader. She was accustomed to taking charge of a goal, mustering the resources to attain it, and then plowing through all obstacles until she achieved it. The intensity of her single minded focus and her incomparable drive made her extraordinary among reformers. These qualities led her to adopt a leadership style that enabled her to accomplish more than most people, although it alienated some reformers. She always insisted that "failure is impossible."

What is most enduring about Anthony's legacy is the rock solid power of her unshakable certitude that national women's suffrage would usher in a new enlightenment. Susan B. Anthony created a whole new world for women and men. She laid the foundation for women to stand on equal grounds with men, to receive equal pay, to make marriage a choice and not an obligation, and to make it possible for women to rule in politics. She has laid the foundation for a future female president in the United States.

Shirley Chisholm

First African American Woman to Run for President

In 1972, Shirley Chisholm was the first African American woman ever to seek a presidential nomination from a major political party.

- Born on November 30, 1924

- First African American woman elected to Congress in 1968

- First African American woman to serve in the House of Representatives

- On January 25, 1972, became the first major party black candidate for President of the United States and the first woman to run for the Democratic presidential nomination

- Died on January 1, 2005

*S*hirley Chisholm paved the way for many African Americans to register and vote for the first time in their lives. Many women, who had left politics to men, took active roles in the political process. She created a major stepping stone in paving the path for minority women to enter politics.

The story of Shirley Chisholm proved that a little girl from Brooklyn, whose parents could not afford to buy a home, could dare to dream of becoming the number one tenant of the White House. Shirley had been right: America was changing.

Birth and Family Background

Shirley Anita St. Hill was born in 1924. Her immigrant parents were from British Guiana and Barbados. When Shirley was three years old her parents Charles and Ruby sent her and her younger sisters to Barbados to live on their grandmother's farm. It was hard for Charles to earn a solid living on the meager salary he made as a baker's helper. Shirley's parents wanted to buy a house, and they wanted their daughters to have proper schooling. They thought letting Grandmother Emily help raise their children was a way to save money they needed and a chance to give Shirley and her sisters a good education.

At an early age, Shirley developed a good work ethic, helping her Grandmother on farm chores. Life in the Barbados farm was simple and they had the basic necessities. Shirley and her sisters never complained about not having luxuries, but appreciated the life that their grandmother could afford them.

Shirley was ten years old when she and her sisters returned to Brooklyn. Their father had a new job, working long hours in a burlap factory. When Shirley was about twelve years old, she and her family moved to a predominantly African American neighborhood of Brooklyn. To make ends meet Shirley's mother took a job as a maid. This meant that Shirley had to help take care of her younger sisters. It was her responsibility to walk her sisters home for lunch and after school each day. Thereafter, she looked after her sisters while her parents worked. Her family depended on her. At an early age, she learned about responsibility and taking care of others. Sometimes, in order to be there for her younger siblings, this called for a sacrifice of her own needs and wants, which would come into play in her later years as a community activist.

Both Shirley's parents encouraged her to visit the Brooklyn Public Library to learn about African American men and women who had devoted themselves to the struggle for racial justice. The library became a friend to Shirley. There, she took a special interest in Harriet Tubman, who led so many slaves to freedom along the Underground Railroad. Harriet Tubman's accomplishments showed Shirley that women could be leaders and that a single woman could lead legions of people, even when a mountain of obstacles stood in her way.

While growing up in Brooklyn, Shirley had been aware of racial differences and prejudice. She lived in neighborhoods with both Black and White people, but she knew that everyone was not treated equally. Meeting Eleanor Roosevelt at age fourteen created a lasting impression on Chisholm. She took to heart Mrs. Roosevelt's advice: "Don't let anybody stand in your way." Here was an example of one strong woman influencing a fourteen-year-old girl to become even stronger and break the barriers hindering a woman's path forward.

After finishing junior high school, Shirley enrolled in Girl's High School. There were some students, however, who teased Shirley for her West Indian accent. She spoke differently from many people in Brooklyn and sometimes they laughed at her for it. Shirley ignored their petty remarks and spent her time reading. Early on, Shirley got used to the idea of being teased and laughed at, and not fitting in with the rest of the group. Shirley was always the "other."

After graduating from Girl's High School in Brooklyn, Shirley enrolled at Brooklyn College. Here, Shirley was exposed to people from all kinds of backgrounds, but there were a very small number of African American students. During her second year at Brooklyn College, Shirley joined the Harriet Tubman Society, a civil rights club whose members met regularly to discuss ways to lessen the racial tensions between Black and White people. Shirley had lots of good ideas for helping African Americans to gain equality. Shirley's friends, both Black and White, began to point out her talent for encouraging others, organizing groups, speaking in public, and putting her ideas into action. She had a skill for oratory and she developed it. In 1949, she married Conrad Chisholm, whom she met at Columbia University. The couple settled in Brooklyn. She became Shirley Chisholm.

NAACP and the Civil Rights Movement

Through campus politics and her work with the National Association for the Advancement of Colored People (NAACP), an organization that was formed in 1909 to work for equal rights for African Americans, Chisholm found a way to voice her opinions about economic and social structures in a rapidly changing nation. She became politically active with the Democratic Party and quickly developed a reputation as a person who challenged the traditional roles of women, African Americans, and the poor.

"I don't measure America by its achievement, but by its potential."

The American Civil Rights Movement was ripe in the mid-1960s. Across the nation, activists were working for equal civil rights for all Americans, regardless of race. In many states, Black people still had to use separate waiting areas in doctors' offices and train stations. They even had to use separate water fountains. In addition, some African Americans were refused their voting rights through various methods. Sometimes, they had to take unfair tests before they could vote. Chisholm felt the discrimination.

"You don't make progress by standing on the sidelines, whimpering and complaining. You make progress by implementing ideas."

Shirley used her power to voice the opinion of many people. She earned a reputation for asking hard, even embarrassing questions. At political club meetings, she questioned such issues as why garbage wasn't picked up on schedule in her neighborhood even though it was properly picked up in White neighborhoods. She also did not hesitate to take her complaints to City Hall. She often led protests to express that her community in Brooklyn was being treated unfairly.

With the Vietnam War raging overseas, Chisholm protested the amount of money being spent for the defense budget while social programs suffered. Chisholm argued that money should not be spent for war while many Americans were hungry, poorly educated, and without adequate housing.

In 1964, Chisholm was elected to the General Assembly of New York State. She accepted it, saying, "Service is the rent that you pay for room on this earth."

First African American Woman in Congress

In 1968, Shirley Chisholm ran as the Democratic candidate for New York's 12th District congressional seat and was elected to the House of Representatives. Defeating Republican candidate James Farmer, Chisholm became the first Black woman elected to Congress. Her campaign slogan was: "Vote Chisholm for Congress: Unbought and Unbossed." She shook voters' hands on street corners and in stores. She attended small get-togethers and spread a message of hope. She knew that the recent assassinations of Martin Luther King and John F. Kennedy had shaken people. She assured them that she would fight for the voters' interests and try to make a difference in Washington.

On June 18, 1968, the Democratic Primary votes were counted. Chisholm won, but by a margin of fewer than eight hundred votes. Addressing her supporters at her campaign headquarters, Chisholm promised: "I know that as a freshman in Congress, I am supposed to be seen and not heard, but my voice will be heard. I have no intention of being quiet."

Once she was in Washington D.C., Chisholm wasted no time in learning how Congress works. She met other members of the House of Representatives and although some were welcoming, others couldn't believe she was there. Once again, she could relate to her childhood years when she was ridiculed and cornered by others, but her resilience and ability to stand up for herself would come into play. She once remembered how one male congressman constantly commented on her salary. He was amazed that a Black woman could make the same amount as he did. Another congressman had a habit of spitting into his handkerchief each time he saw her. One day, she came up behind him quietly, pulled out a handkerchief, and spit into it loudly. "Beat you today," she said. Suddenly, his habit stopped.

Shirley would serve in Congress for a total of seven terms, from 1968 to 1982. As a congresswoman, Shirley worked hard on behalf of her district. She helped people find jobs. She fought discrimination and spoke out for the rights of poor people and children.

"As a Black person, I am no stranger to race and prejudice, but the truth is that in the political world I have been far oftener discriminated against because I am a woman than because I am Black."

While she was in Congress, Chisholm focused on concerns she thought were specific to African Americans and women. Since there were so few African Americans in the House of Representatives, many Blacks throughout the country approached her with their problems and issues. They knew she could relate to them. Women's rights activists also saw Chisholm as an ally and sought out her support.

Shirley Chisholm used her power to voice the opinion of many people. In 1968, she was the first black woman elected to Congress.

Chisholm quickly took on her new responsibilities. In doing so, she offered many ideas, one of which led to the Search for Education, Elevation, and Knowledge (SEEK) program that provided college scholarships for minority students. She also sponsored a bill that helped domestic workers. Remembering that her mother worked as a maid, Chisholm knew that domestic workers sometimes lost their jobs and then had no income until they could find new ones. In 1965, it became law that employers of domestic workers had to pay for unemployment insurance. This enabled workers to receive money if they had to find new jobs.

Shirley also spoke against traditional roles for women professionals, including secretaries, teachers, and librarians, arguing that women were capable of entering many other professions. Black women, especially, she felt, had been pushed into stereotypical roles or conventional professions, such as maids and nannies. Chisholm supported the idea that they needed to escape, not just by governmental aid, but also by self effort.

Chisholm also sponsored bills that provided state aid to day care centers and raised the amount of money that local school districts could spend. In addition, she helped pass legislation that protected female teachers. Before, when a teacher took maternity leave, she lost her tenure. This meant that when she returned to her position, she was treated as a beginner. In 1965, a new law ensured that female teachers could keep their tenure and years of experience after maternity leave.

Another controversial issue was the idea of equal rights for women. Throughout the United States, women argued that they should be allowed the same opportunities as men and be paid the same for doing the same jobs. Chisholm addressed the House of Representatives in support of the Equal Rights Amendment. She pointed out that women made up more than half the U.S. population, but they held only two percent of managerial positions in the country. The Equal Rights Amendment never passed. However, women have made great strides in attaining equality in the decades since Chisholm made this speech.

Presidential Campaign

Shirley Chisholm decided to run for President in 1972. She was the first African American woman ever to seek a presidential nomination from a major political party. When she announced her candidacy, she stated:

> *"I am not the candidate of Black America, although I am Black and proud. I am not the candidate for the women's movement of this country, although I am a woman…I am the candidate of the people."*

During her bid for the Democratic Party's presidential nomination, Shirley survived three assassination attempts. Though she did not get the nomination, Shirley did not see that loss as a defeat. The fact that she had entered the race alone was a victory to her. In her biography *The Good Fight*, Chisholm reflected back to her 1972 campaign:

> *"I ran because someone had to do it first. In this country everybody is supposed to be able to run for President, but that's never really been true. I ran because most people think the country is not ready for a Black candidate, not ready for a woman candidate. Someday…"*

After her unsuccessful presidential campaign, Chisholm continued to serve in the U.S. House of Representatives for another decade. She announced her retirement from Congress in 1982. As a member of the Black Caucus, which is a group of lawmakers who represent African Americans, she

"As a Black person, I am no stranger to race and prejudice, but the truth is that in the political world I have been far oftener discriminated against because I am a woman than because I am Black."

was able to watch Black representation in the Congress grow and welcome other Black female congresswomen. Chisholm retired to Florida, where she died on January 1, 2005.

The Strides She Made

Chisholm is a model of independence and honesty and has championed several issues including civil rights, aid for the poor, and women's rights. Although Chisholm broke ground as the nation's first Black congresswoman and the first Black presidential candidate, she has said she would rather be remembered for continuing throughout her life to fight for rights for women and African Americans.

As an African American woman, Shirley Chisholm allowed no one to stand in her way. She fought for what she believed in, even though, it did not ensure a victory every time. For Chisholm, it was not always about winning, but about making a statement.

She was spat at by other politicians, survived assassination attempts, and suffered economic hardships, yet Shirley Chisholm kept her head high and worked for women's rights. It wasn't long before others took Shirley's lead. Shirley Chisholm paved the way for Geraldine Ferraro in 1984 and Hillary Clinton and Sarah Palin in 2008.

Some people thought that a Black person would never be elected president of the United States, but Shirley Chisholm always knew that it was possible. Her efforts paved the way for more people to try. Chisholm once said:

"I do not want to be remembered as the first Black woman to be elected to the United States Congress, even though I am. I do not want to be remembered as the first woman who happened to be Black to make a serious bid for the presidency. I'd like to be known as a catalyst for change... The time has come to change America. Someday, somewhere, somehow, someone other than a White male could be President."

Marie Curie

Physicist and Chemist Famous for her Work in Radioactivity

When Marie Curie was four years old, her mother contracted tuberculosis, resulting in her never being able to kiss or hug her mother. This partly explains her estrangement from people in her adult years.

- · Born on November 7, 1867

- · Developed techniques for isolating radioactive isotopes

- · Discovered Polonium and Radium

- · First woman to win a Nobel Prize

- · Only woman to win the Nobel Prize in two different fields

- · Only woman to win the award in multiple sciences

- · First female professor at the University of Paris

- · Died of radiation in July 4, 1934

Marie Curie was a Polish-born French physicist and chemist famous for her work on radioactivity. In 1893, she became the first woman to secure a degree in physics at The Sorbonne. She was also the first woman to win a Nobel Prize and she is the only woman to win the award in multiple sciences, in physics and chemistry. Her achievements include the creation of a theory of radioactivity, techniques for isolating radioactive isotopes, and the discovery of two new elements, Polonium and Radium. She was the first woman to be elected to the 224-year-old French Academy of Medicine. In addition to having a spectacular career, Marie raised two daughters, largely as a single mother, and saw that they were well educated and independent.

Marie Curie suffered great sadness and hardship in her life. Even so, she never lost sight of her dream. She was driven by a belief in science and progress, hard work, education, and helping others. She lived that dream. Louis Pasteur famously said, "Fortune favors the prepared mind." Major achievements, however, need more than scientific preparedness; they need an individual peculiarly suited to the task. Marie Curie's character, formed by discrimination and deprivation, by parental pressure, personal ambition, and patriotism, was such an individual.

Family Financial and Health Struggles

Marie Skłodowska Curie came from a brilliant, hard-working family of physicists. She was born Maria Skłodowska in Warsaw, Poland, where she lived until she was twenty-four years old. Her mother, Bronislawa, was a devout Catholic, but her husband was not so religious. He was a scientist.

The family had lost its property and fortunes through patriotic involvements in Polish national uprisings. This condemned Marie, her elder sisters, and brother to a difficult struggle to get ahead in life. Both her parents were teachers who believed deeply in the importance of education. Marie had her first lessons in physics and chemistry from her father.

Financial hardship was an ever present theme in the family. When money was short Bronislawa learned how to make and repair shoes for children. She was a practical woman and was never ashamed to turn her hand to hard work. Maria acquired this hard work ethic.

In 1871, when Marie was four years old, her mother began to lose weight. She coughed constantly, a classic sign of tuberculosis. Marie was never to remember a mother's kiss or caress. Although she may have felt that physically distancing herself from the child would protect her from tuberculosis, it had another less desirable effect on the small girl. Even though her mother smiled and gave her affectionate looks, these signs represented mixed messages to Marie. It was difficult for the youngster to understand the lack of physical contact from a mother who professed a great love for her. Marie worshipped her mother, but when she pushed her clinging hands aside and suggested that she go outside to play in the garden she felt rejected. These childhood experiences may explain why as she grew older she found it very difficult to be physically close to people. Human contact was absent in her early years.

Sometimes the family rented out rooms to students to help pay the bills. At first there were five, then ten, and then twenty renters. In these quarters, there was little privacy. Marie slept on a couch in the dining room. Each morning, she rose at six to set the table for breakfast. In January 1876, one of their boarders brought more than books when he came to stay. He was a carrier of typhus, a deadly disease that can be spread by contaminated lice. Two of Marie's sisters, Bronislawa and Sophia, caught the disease.... Fourteen-year-old Sophia died.

Mrs. Skłodowska, too weak from tuberculosis to leave the house and accompany her family to the funeral, watched from the window as her daughter's coffin was carried down the street. Marie, dressed in her dead sister's long black coat, walked behind the coffin as if in a trance. This was the first coffin she would follow; and it would not be the last. The hardships she endured as a child influenced the kind of adult that she became.

Mrs. Skłodowska's condition worsened. On May 9, 1878, Marie's mother died. Marie was ten at the time. Although she continued to go to church with her family as she had done before, something had changed for Marie. Deep inside she rejected the faith her mother had cherished. For the rest of her life, she never maintained any kind of religious belief. Science would take that place.

After Bronislawa died, joy and laughter were rare in the household. Marie's father mourned his wife's death by becoming preoccupied with his work. The period of mourning lasted for several years, as was the custom in Poland. The windows had black curtains, family members wore black veils, and notepaper was edged with black. The atmosphere was not a very healthy one for a sensitive young girl and the death of two family members had permanently left a mark of profound depression on her life, the beginning of a pattern that would remain with her all her life. Mentally, Marie prepared for a difficult life.

Marie became an introvert. Books were her escape and solace from her sorrowful existence. She spoke little. She started to love herself less and became selfless. Out of this depression was born a strong woman who made it her mission to work tirelessly and do good for her family and society.

"Life is not easy for any of us. But what of that? We must have perseverance and above all confidence in ourselves. We must believe that we are gifted for something and that this thing must be attained."

Education would have to become the way out of the family's financial shackles, but women in Poland were not allowed to attend college in their own country. However, there were no laws in Poland to prevent her from leaving the country for an education. Marie's dream was to study at The Sorbonne. Her father was unable to educate his daughter's because his money was being drained to pay for his son, Jozef's, medical education.

Marie Curie had big dreams. She also knew what it would take to achieve that dream. All her energy was invested to making that dream come true.

At eighteen, Bronya, Marie's elder sister, assumed the role of her mother, but longed to be a physician like her brother. Marie wanted to be a scientist or at least become "something," by which she meant a person of importance in the world. To solve the problem, Marie and her elder sister, Bronya, came to an arrangement: Marie should go to work as a governess and help her sister with the money she managed to save so that Bronya could study medicine at The Sorbonne. When Bronya had taken her degree, she, in turn, would contribute to the cost of Marie's studies at The Sorbonne. Marie became a governess to pay for her sister's education and her sister kept her part of the promise once she became a doctor.

Going to Sorbonne

In 1891, at age twenty-four and almost penniless, Marie began her education at The Sorbonne in Paris. She learned that if she had enough patience and tenacity, the seemingly impossible could be accomplished. The room was so cold in the winter that the water froze in the basin. She slept beneath all her clothes piled on the bed. Sometimes she varied her diet of tea, chocolate, bread, and fruit with an occasional egg or meat, but not often. Her attic room was without heat, lighting, and water. She had a stove for heating and a petroleum oil lamp for reading at night. Marie nearly starved during the first months by herself. Not surprisingly she fainted and often became ill.

"We should be interested in things, not persons," she later wrote, indicating how she coped with emotional deprivation. All this enabled her to ignore such obstacles as sexual discrimination, lack of money, and her inadequate preparation in chemistry and physics. However, each time she recalled these two and a half years of "deprivation," she pronounced them "one of the best memories of my life." When she graduated, she had the highest grades in the class. Marie had achieved her dream of study, of liberty, of independence.

"All my mind was centered on my studies. I divided my time between courses, experimental work, and study in the library. In the evening I worked in my room, sometimes very late into the night. All that I saw and learned was a new delight to me. It was like a new world open to me, the world of science which I was at last permitted to know in all liberty," Marie recalled.

Marie Meets Pierre Curie

In 1894, Pierre Curie entered her life. He was an instructor at the School of Physics and Chemistry, the École Supérieure de Physique et de Chimie Industrielles de la Ville de Paris (ESPCI). It was their mutual interest in magnetism that drew Marie Skłodowska and Curie together.

Almost a year later, in July 1895, Marie and Pierre Curie married, and thereafter the two physicists hardly ever left their laboratory. They shared two hobbies, long bicycle trips and journeys abroad, which brought them even closer. Pierre wrote, "We dreamed of living in the world quite removed from human beings," and this was a key to both their personalities. Her daughter Eve wrote that both her parents were made for isolation and were happiest living this "anti natural" existence. Her early research, together with her husband, were often performed under difficult conditions, laboratory arrangements were poor and both had to undertake much teaching to earn a livelihood.

Marie brought to her marriage the same ardor that she had for science. She studied domestic skills as if they were scientific proposals. The student who had not known how to make soup now made gooseberry jelly. At thirty, she was pregnant, late in those days for bearing a first child. Marie found herself coping with a heavy workload coupled with childcare. At lunchtime and in the evening Marie would rush home to nurse her daughter, Irene. Her life of juggling motherhood, scientific work, and continuous financial problems brought back the old patterns of exhaustion and depression. She was so distraught and fragmented that the doctors advised she be sent to a sanatorium, but she would not leave her work, her husband, or her child. Albert Einstein professed deep friendship for Marie, but described her as "cold as a herring."

First Nobel Prize

The discovery of radioactivity by Henri Becquerel in 1896 inspired the Curies in their brilliant research and analyses, which led to the isolation of Polonium, named after the country of Marie's birth, and Radium. In July 1898, Marie and her husband published a paper together, announcing the existence of Polonium.

On December 26, 1898, the Curies announced the existence of a second element, which they named "radium" for its intense radioactivity, a word that they coined. Marie Curie developed methods for the separation of radium from radioactive residues in sufficient quantities to allow for its characterization and the careful study of its properties, therapeutic properties in particular.

Radium would become her colossal achievement, but, in fact, her greatest achievement was in employing an entirely new method to discover elements by measuring their radioactivity. In the next decade, scientists who located the source and composition of radioactivity made more discoveries concerning the atom and its structure than in all the centuries that had gone before.

Marie switched back and forth between being a scientist and a mother. Ten days after Radium's discovery was announced, she noted that Irene had fifteen teeth. Marie earned her doctorate on June 25, 1903. She was the first woman in France to do so.

The discovery of Radium was honored on December 10, 1903, when Marie, Pierre, and Henri Bacquerel were awarded the Nobel Prize. However, only a few weeks afterward, Marie and Pierre's second daughter died shortly after birth. Grief overwhelmed Marie again. While Marie agonized over the loss of her baby, Radium became famous. Marie was in a depressed state. Around the same time she had lost her father also. She was depleted physically and had not fully mourned the loss of her father or child.

The award carried with it a diploma, gold medals, and a cash prize, and it brought them worldwide fame. The Curies, who had always struggled with lack of money, used some of their $20,000 to hire a lab assistant. They also generously gave money to friends and family who were in need. Neither Marie nor Pierre bought even the smallest gift for themselves.

Marie and Pierre could have gotten patents on their Radium and the process they used to extract it. If they had, anyone who used their Radium or their method of extraction would have had to pay money to the Curies. They could have been rich. They could have gone home and never worked another day in their lives.

Marie Curie walking with President Warren G. Harding in 1921.

Instead, the Curies gave Radium away. It proved what great heights could be achieved if greed was removed and if people didn't care who got the credit for achieving greatness. The Curies were more concerned about what they could do for humankind than what humankind could do for them. Said Marie:

"We refused to draw any material profit from our discovery. We took no copyright and published without reserve all the results of our research, as well as the exact processes of the preparation of radium."

"Curie Cures Cancer"

When it was learned that Radium could be used to treat cancer, the entire world was suddenly interested in it. "Curie Cures Cancer" — this headline appeared in newspapers across America. This claim alleviated a fear of death and struck a deep chord in America's collective psyche. The first recorded successful use of Radium treatments to cure cancer happened in St. Petersburg, where two patients suffering from basal cell carcinoma of the face were successfully treated. Although the scientific world was slowly becoming aware of the efficacy of Radium treatment, its use was extremely limited.

Marie Curie tried to rein in the mythic image she had helped form. She warned that the "Curie therapy," i.e., radiation treatments, provided no sure cure for cancer. "I am one of those who think like Nobel, that humanity will draw more good than evil from new discoveries," she said.

In June 1903, Pierre was invited to London to give a lecture on Radium at the Royal Institution. Since Marie was a woman, she could not speak to the all-male group. No woman before Marie had ever been permitted even to attend a lecture there. The Royal Institution made an exception for Marie since she was the co-discoverer of Radium. She was allowed to sit in the audience.

After they won the Nobel Prize, news reports about and photographs of the Curies spread all over the world. Their story captured the interest of people everywhere: "A poor Polish woman beat all odds to get an education in Paris; she fell in love with a renowned scientist and worked with him for four years in a pitiful shed where they discovered a new element, which could be used to treat cancer; and then they won a Nobel Prize." Marie and Pierre were suddenly famous; they disliked it tremendously.

The Curies had extra money for the first time in Marie's life. Marie remembered Madame Kozlowska, one of her childhood teachers. Madame Kozlowska, who was French, had married a Polish man and had lived in Poland ever since. Marie recalled how her teacher longed to see her beloved France again, but could not afford to travel there. Madame Kozlowska yearned for France, just as Marie had for Poland. Marie provided Madame Kozlowska with the trip of her dreams. She paid her travel expenses to and from France and invited her to stay in the Curie home during her visit. Marie never forgot a kindness that had been done for her or, for that matter, a wrong that had been done to her. She also knew that she did not make it alone; people like Madame Kozlowska had helped her.

Meanwhile, Marie and Pierre's work with Radium continued to affect their health. Pierre said to a friend: "To tell the truth, I can only keep up by avoiding all physical fatigue. And my wife is in the same condition; we can no longer dream of the great work days of times gone by."

In 1904, Marie gave birth to another daughter. When women asked how she was able to balance a family and a scientific career, Marie answered: "It has not been easy; it required a great deal of decision and of self sacrifice."

Second Nobel Prize

In 1911, Curie became the first and only woman to win a second Nobel Prize for the discovery of the two new elements, polonium and radium. She earned, on her own, the award in chemistry for isolating pure Radium. She was the first person honored with two Nobel Prizes. Curie's second Nobel Prize enabled her to talk the French government into funding the building of a private Radium Institute (Institut du radium, now the Institut Curie), which was built in 1914 and at which research was conducted in chemistry, physics, and medicine. The Institute became a haven of Nobel Prize winners.

"Be less curious about people and more curious about ideas."

Pierre's Death

Pierre was killed in an accident in 1906, leaving Marie grief-stricken. Her second daughter had just turned one. After Pierre died, Marie forbade the children to ever mention his name again. Rather than talking about it and dealing with the grieving process, she shut herself completely from the outside world. Her mind functioned on a different plane. Coping with emotional tragedy was too painful for Marie. The laboratory had become Marie's safe harbor, the one place where she could endure life without Pierre. Pierre's death marked a defining moment in her life. She became an incurably lonely woman. With Pierre's death, Marie irrevocably closed to the world.

The French government offered her a pension, but she refused to take the money. She was thirty-nine years old at the time. Marie declined the pension, saying: "I don't want a pension. I am young enough to earn my living and that of my children."

Marie took Pierre's place as Professor of General Physics in the Faculty of Sciences, at The Sorbonne, the first time a woman had held this position. She was also appointed Director of the Curie Laboratory in the Radium Institute of the University of Paris, founded in 1914. Andrew Carnegie, the wealthy Pittsburgh philanthropist, founded the Curie Scholarships in 1907 with $50,000, which would pay the salaries for additional staff to assist Marie in her laboratory work.

"Nothing in life is to be feared, it is only to be understood. Now is the time to understand more, so that we may fear less."

X-Ray Machines in World War 1

Throughout her life, Marie Curie actively promoted the use of Radium to alleviate suffering during World War I. Assisted by her daughter, Irene, she personally devoted herself to this humanitarian work. Since the discovery of x-rays, it was possible to "see" inside the body without surgery to detect broken bones or the location of bullets. Marie understood that the ability to take x-rays of soldiers quickly after their injuries could often mean the difference between life and death. Although she had taught and lectured about x-rays, she had never worked with them herself. First, she learned how to take x-rays; and then she taught others. The problem was that there were few x-ray machines, and most of them were only in major hospitals. X-ray equipment needed to be brought closer to the battlefield.

Marie devised the idea of mobile x-ray units that could be used in battlefront hospitals. Bullets and shrapnel could be located with x-rays to help doctors treat wounded soldiers. Each mobile unit contained a small generator that could be hooked up to a car battery when electricity was unavailable onsite. An x-ray tube was installed on a movable stand so that it could easily be wheeled to the crucial area. There was a folding table for the patient, photographic plates, a screen, heavy curtains to exclude light, and ampules filed with radon. These were called the "Petites Curies." She used Irene as the driver. Soldiers were carried into the makeshift medical tent: Some were dead, some had missing limbs, and some had shattered bones and shrapnel wounds. Marie trained 150 women to become x-ray technicians. Their operators took more than one million x-ray images, saving countless lives.

Promptly after the war started, Marie had donated the gold Nobel Prize medals she and her husband had been awarded to the war effort.

Death

Marie Curie visited Poland for the last time in the spring of 1934. Only a few months later, on July 4, 1934, she died at the Sancellemoz Sanatorium in Passy, in Haute-Savoie, Eastern France, from aplastic anemia, contracted from exposure to radiation. The damaging effects of ionizing radiation were not then known and much of her work had been carried out in a shed without proper safety measures. She had carried test tubes containing radioactive isotopes in her pocket and stored them in her desk drawer, remarking on the pretty blue-green light that the substances gave off in the dark.

Even as she lay on her deathbed, Marie insisted that a dose of fresh air might be all that was needed to help her recover. With the persistence that had allowed her to perform seemingly impossible tasks, Marie Curie never acknowledged that her beloved radium might have betrayed her.

A frequently asked question is, "How could her denial have been so strong? How could the Curies expose themselves, their associates, and even their precious daughter Irene and her husband to the devastating effects of radiation?" It was love. Along with love was Marie's intense belief that great scientific discoveries demanded sacrifice. From childhood she had been inculcated with the theory that deprivation and disregard for personal welfare in the service of a great cause were noble characteristics.

The Strides She Made

Marie Curie's life was truly inspirational. Many people have benefited from the discoveries made by Marie Curie. The radiation which burned her skin as she worked with it, eventually came to be used to kill cancer cells in patients suffering from the disease.

If the work of Marie Curie helped overturn established ideas in physics and chemistry, it has had an equally profound effect in the societal sphere. To attain her scientific achievements, she had to overcome barriers that were placed in her way because she was a woman, in both her native and her adoptive country. Women of Marie's day had few rights. They were not allowed to vote and just to open a bank account they needed their husband's approval. Marie was often way ahead of her male counterparts, yet, many of them would never accept her as a serious scientist because of her gender. Although Marie was opening doors of opportunities for women in science who would come after her, she was not a feminist or crusader for women's rights. All she cared about was her work, and she thought of herself as a scientist, not as a woman scientist.

Marie is remembered as a scientific Joan of Arc. Paris streets are named after Madame Curie and her husband, Pierre; the French 500-franc-note, now a collector's item, is imprinted with her face and her so called "miserable shed" laboratory. Albert Einstein is reported to have remarked that she was probably the only person who was not corrupted by the fame that she had won.

Many women have been inspired by Marie Curie, this brave woman who defied the strictures against her sex. She has been lauded as proof that women can do it all and perfectly. She was emancipated, independent, and uncorrupted. The perception abides that, in addition to having a spectacular career, she was a model mother for her two daughters, far ahead of her time in emphasizing the importance of a strong body, a good education, and an unfettered view of life. She was ahead of her time.

Amelia Earhart

First Woman to Fly Solo Across the Atlantic

During an attempt to make a round-the-world flight of the globe in 1937, Amelia Earhart disappeared over the central Pacific Ocean. Fascination with her life, career, and disappearance continues to this day.

- Born July 24, 1897
- First aviatrix to fly solo across the Atlantic Ocean
- First woman to fly across the continental US and back again
- First pilot to fly solo from the Hawaiian Islands over the Pacific to California, and therefore, the first woman to fly over the Atlantic and the Pacific
- Pioneering advocate of women
- During an attempt to make a round-the-world flight of the globe in 1937, Earhart disappeared over the central Pacific Ocean. Fascination with her life, career and disappearance continues this day.
- Declared legally dead January 5, 1939

*A*melia Earhart disappeared while attempting to be the first woman to fly around the world in 1937. Yet, she remains America's foremost female flier and a feminist icon. In 1928, she became the first woman to fly across the Atlantic; four years later, she became the first woman to fly it solo at a time when only one other person, Charles Lindbergh, had done so. Subsequently, she performed any number of aviation "firsts," many of which were also "first woman" records.

Amelia Earhart was an early symbol of women's emergence as individuals in their own right and a pioneering advocate of women having careers other than as wives and mothers. As a woman, she always pushed herself to establish new records and attain new heights. The thought of exploring unchartered territories as a woman never deterred her.

Aviation was an expensive pursuit. Financial difficulties forced Amelia to push her flying dreams aside from her life and take on any job that came along her way. This changed when she received a phone call while working as a social worker in Massachusetts. It was a phone call that changed her life.

Birth and Family Background

Amelia Mary Earhart, daughter of Samuel Edwin Stanton Earhart and Amelia "Amy" Otis Earhart, was born in Atchison, Kansas. The small town of Atchison seemed an unlikely birthplace for a woman whose name, more than fifty years after her death, remains synonymous with adventure, heroism, and posthumous mystery. As a child, Earhart spent long hours playing in the outdoors, climbing trees, hunting rats with a rifle and "belly-slamming" her sled downhill. She was a tomboy.

Because her father's work often required him to travel away from home and his wife Amy liked to accompany him, Amelia and her sister frequently spent time at the home of their wealthy grandparents. Their grandfather was a well-respected judge.

Amelia's father paid the way for the family to visit the 1904 World's Fair in St. Louis, Missouri. On their return from the fair, the seven-year-old Amelia designed and built a roller coaster in the yard, with long planks propped against the roof shed. Traveling much faster than anticipated, she raced past the other children in a blur, bruising her self. Such tomboyish games were very much to Amelia's taste. Early on, she showed signs of experimenting with new ideas, breaking away from traditional feminine activities, and finding fun in doing what she loved.

Moving to Iowa

Edwin Earhart's job led to a transfer to Des Moines, Iowa. At the age of ten, Earhart saw her first aircraft at the Iowa State Fair in Des Moines, five years after the Wright Brothers had made their epic flight on the dunes of Kitty Hawk. Her first impressions of an airplane were dim.

In 1908, the Earhart children were enrolled in public school for the first time, with Amelia entering the seventh grade at the age of twelve. At first, the move to Des Moines seemed like a blessing for the Earharts, as it doubled the father's salary. Amelia recalled happy evenings when her father would read aloud or tell fascinating stories he made up on the spot. Father and daughter also shared a love of music, especially the piano.

This happy time was, unfortunately, a prelude to a period that saw the loss of their material prosperity and the beginning of the disintegration of the family. As Edwin's alcoholism progressed, it interfered with his career and family life. Amelia's grandmother died in 1911, leaving an estate reputedly valued at a million dollars to be equally divided between the four surviving children. Fearing that Edwin's drinking would drain the funds, Amy's share of her inheritance was locked into a trust for twenty years, or until Edwin's death, whichever came first.

Growing up with a father who drank left Amelia with many dark incidents that she would have liked to forget. The arguments in the home, the embarrassing incidents, the inconsistency of emotional attachment, and the dysfunctional family relationships left dark memories. Yet, she loved her father. Amelia's mother pointed fingers at her husband due to his lack of financial funds. Amy felt that she deserved more financially. Amelia would break this cycle. Rather than following in her mother's footsteps of blaming her male counterpart for lack of finances, Amelia actually did whatever came along her way to make money; as a social worker, as a photographer, as an author, and, finally, as an aviatrix. Amelia felt that earning money and seeking independence was a critical part of becoming an independent woman.

As Amelia entered her teens, it became more and more apparent that her parent's marriage was no longer a happy one. Edwin's constant battle with alcoholism would soon split the family apart. The family also struggled financially. Soon the amenities of life had to be sacrificed for the necessities of existence. Amelia's sister wrote: "The hardship and mental suffering that Amelia and I endured as adolescents made an indelible impression upon us and help to explain some of Amelia's actions and attitudes in her later life."

Amy took the children to Chicago, leaving Edwin behind. She enrolled Amelia at Hyde Park High School, where Amelia became a loner. When she graduated from high school in 1916, Amelia deliberately missed the celebrations. Her graduating class photograph was suitably captioned: "The girl in brown who walks alone." She was a lonely girl who preferred to go solo.

"In soloing, as in other activities, it is far easier to start something than it is to finish it."

World War 1 and Red Cross

World War 1 had been raging in Europe since 1914. In April 1917, the United States entered the conflict. Earhart saw the returning wounded soldiers and, after receiving training as a nurse's aide from the Red Cross, she began working with the Volunteer Aid Detachment at Spadina Military Hospital. Her duties included preparing food in the kitchen for patients with special diets and handing out prescribed medication in the hospital's dispensary. No doubt Amelia heard about their adventures in the air while tending to their injuries. Amelia began visiting the airfield whenever she could to watch the pilots' training maneuvers. The stories that injured pilots told about flying made her want to be a pilot, too.

In 1919, Amelia Earhart enrolled in premed classes at Columbia University at a time when most women wanted nothing more than to finish college, get married, and raise a family. However, within a few months, she realized that she did not want to be a physician.

After moving to California, Amelia drove with her father to an aerial meet in Long Beach on December 28, 1920. On this occasion, she thought she might like to fly. She asked her father to inquire about the cost of flying lessons. Her father found out that it cost about $1,000 to learn to fly. He booked a flight for her the following day. He paid ten dollars for his daughter to be taken up as a passenger for a ten-minute flight. This ten-dollar flight forever changed Earhart's life.

"By the time I had gotten two or three hundred feet off the ground," she said, "I knew I had to fly."

There was no sudden dramatic change, but there was a new sense of awareness of herself and a new determination in her actions. She had found a direction and, unlike previous interests, this one was to last. With characteristic enthusiasm, Amelia now became more and more obsessed with flying. In time, aviation not only became a raison d'etre, but also a means of escape from an increasingly troubled home life and constant squabbles between her parents about money. The sky was the place where she could be herself.

Beginning Flying Lessons

Working at a variety of jobs, including selling sausages, working in a photography lab, and as a stenographer at the local telephone company, as well as driving a truck, she managed to save $1,000 for flying lessons. "Flying might not be all plain sailing, but the fun of it is worth the price," Amelia said.

Amelia's first solo fight ended almost before it began. A shock absorber broke off during takeoff, causing the plane's left wing to sag. Failure did not dissuade her form pursuing her dreams. This accident motivated her even more to fly again. Amelia continued to fly solo whenever she had enough money to pay for the fuel. In addition, she participated in a few air rodeos. Though Amelia was not particularly interested in impressing air show crowds, the money she earned helped pay for her aviation expenses and, as a female pilot, she was also aware of the publicity factor. In nearly all of her future endeavors, Amelia tried to promote the abilities of women. Money, or the lack thereof, never stopped her from achieving her dreams. She aimed high.

On May 15, 1923, Earhart became the sixteenth woman to be issued a pilot's license (#6017) by the Fédération Aéronautique Internationale. Using part of her mother's inheritance, for her twenty-fourth birthday in 1921, Amelia bought a "Kinner Airster," which she named Amelia.

Amelia loved flying. Yet, she also knew that her mother's inheritance had been rapidly dwindling and her aviation expenses contributed to her parent's financial situation. Amelia sold her plane and took on additional jobs. Financial difficulties forced her to push aside her flying dreams, at least temporarily. By 1924, her parents had divorced.

Social Worker

Soon after, she found employment as a teacher. In 1926, she became a social worker at Denison House in Medford, Massachusetts. By May 1, 1927, Charles Lindbergh became the first pilot to fly the Atlantic nonstop. As a Boston resident and licensed pilot, Amelia joined the local chapter of the National Aeronautic Association. She was the only woman in a sea of men.

"There is no door closed to ability, so when women are ready there will be opportunity for them in aviation."

Amelia found being a social worker "too confining" and the pay insufficient. She still yearned to fly, but with no regular income her opportunities to do so were limited.

It was in 1928, right after Lindbergh's flight, that Amelia's life changed forever. She was helping to organize a class play where she was teaching English at the time when the telephone rang.

"I am too busy now," she said. "Ask whoever is calling to call again later."

Pressed, she went to the phone "very unwillingly" and heard a masculine voice introduce himself.

"Hello. You don't know me, but my name is Raley. Captain H. H. Raley. Would you like to fly the Atlantic?"

It was a phone call that changed her life.

First Woman to Fly the Atlantic

Amelia Earhart would only be a passenger, yet the opportunity to become the first woman to fly the Atlantic was exciting. The pilot and navigator was Wilmer "Bill" Stultz. The mechanic was Louis "Slim" Gordon, who knew aircraft engines inside and out. Amelia had been told upfront that Stultz and Gordon would be paid for the flight: Gordon, $5,000, and Stultz, $20,000. She would be paid nothing since she would be traveling only as a passenger. Any money that Amelia received in connection with the flight, such as the profits earned from the first-person newspaper account she was expected to write directly after the trip, were to be returned to help pay for the costs of the flight.

Departure took place on June 3, 1928. Up until then, the flight was kept a secret. Despite the newsworthiness of being the first woman to fly across the Atlantic, Amelia did not feel she deserved any special recognition. After all, it was Bill Stultz and Slim Gordon who had done the work. "I was just a baggage, like a sack of potatoes," she said. "Maybe someday I'll try it alone."

By this time, news agencies were reporting on several women pilots who were hoping to be the first to fly solo across the Atlantic. While Amelia outwardly denied any interest in making the same trip, she was secretly formulating her plans.

Charles Lindbergh's wife, Anne, said the following of Amelia: "She is the most amazing person, just as tremendous as C., I think. It startles me how much alike they are. Charles doesn't realize it, but he hasn't talked to her as much. She has the clarity of mind, impersonal eye, coolness of temperament, balance of a scientist."

Attracting Publicity

Probably to the distress of her more stuffy relatives, Amelia's name started to appear in the newspapers with a regularity that indicates Amelia not only recognized the value of publicity, but also was not averse to it. In 1923, a newspaper article appeared in the *New York Times* with Amelia in a flying dress. Certain older family members were not pleased with this publicity and one uncle in particular wrote to Amelia to complain that it was simply not done. "The only time a lady's name should appear in print is at her birth, her marriage, and her funeral," this uncle told her.

"Woman to fly for Cedar Hill Fete," proclaimed one. "Miss Amelia Earhart flies in a plane over Boston" said another. *The Boston Globe* interviewed her a few weeks later in June 1927 and she took full advantage of the occasion to promote flying, especially for women. Thereafter, she was often in the columns of the *Globe*, where she was usually described as "one of the best women pilots in the United States."

"Each time we make a choice, we pay with courage to behold the restless day. And count it fair."

Flying the Atlantic Solo

It was in 1928 that George Putnam, a prominent publisher, heard of Amelia's attempt to fly across the Atlantic solo, the first person to try to do so since Lindbergh. No woman had so far flown across, though several women were in advanced preparations, ranging in various degrees of seriousness. He took a keen interest in Amelia, and later, it translated into a romance.

In 1932, at the age of thirty-four, Earhart set off from Harbour Grace, Newfoundland, in an effort to become the first woman to successfully fly alone across the Atlantic. The proposed flight date was set by George Putnam. Amelia would leave five years to the day that Lindbergh had made his flight: May 20-21, 1927.

"Never interrupt someone doing what you said couldn't be done."

Amelia intended to fly to Paris in her single engine Lockheed Vega 5b to emulate Charles Lindbergh's solo flight. Knowing the difficulty of landing on unfamiliar ground in the dark, Amelia preferred to take off at sunset, fly during the night and, with luck, reach her destination during daylight. During the ride, the altimeter, the instrument that records the height above the ground, failed. In all her experience of flying, she had never had this happen before. From this point on, she had no indication of her true height — a vital factor in instrument flying. However, she carried a barograph, which would at least give her an indication of her climb and descent.

"The most difficult thing is the decision to act, the rest is merely tenacity. The fears are paper tigers. You can do anything you decide to do. You can act to change and control your life; and the procedure, the process is its own reward."

About ten hours after take-off, Amelia reached to turn on her reserve tank of fuel and noticed that the cabin fuel gauge had begun to leak. Fuel was dripping steadily into the cockpit and onto Amelia's left shoulder, filling the cabin with fumes. She later recalled deciding, if she even had a choice, that she would rather drown than burn. Instead of turning around and flying four more hours to Newfoundland, she decided to continue onward to Europe.

When she ran into fog, she could no longer chance going low because she might crash into the water. Instead, she soared into the higher, thicker clouds. "It was," she later recalled, "the roughest air I have ever encountered while flying completely blind."

Upon sighting a small fishing boat, Amelia knew she had to be fairly close to shore. After a flight lasting fourteen hours and fifty-six minutes, Earhart landed in a pasture at Culmore, north of Derry, Northern Ireland: She had flown 2,026 miles across the Atlantic — alone. Of her accomplishment, Amelia said:

"Probably my greatest satisfaction was to indicate by example now and then that women can sometimes do things themselves if given the chance."

With her successful solo flight across the Atlantic, Amelia was now not only the first female pilot to accomplish this feat, but she was also the first person — man or woman — to make two transatlantic journeys by air. Amelia had also established a new women's record for making the longest nonstop flight.

The public embraced Amelia as "Lady Lindy," the feminine counterpart of Charles Lindbergh, but more to the point — the flight made her a leading advocate of the air industry and opened the way for more flying distinctions.

There were several good reasons for Amelia wanting to fly the Atlantic solo. First and foremost was a personal need to prove something to herself and the critics who had jeered that she had been merely a passenger on the 1928 flight. Probably her own severest critic, Amelia was well aware that her career had been built on a flight in which she played no active role and it hurt to have this pointed out. In the intervening time, she had learned the craft, become an experienced and competent pilot, and, in a sense, had "earned" her place in the newspapers, yet she wanted and needed to prove that she was the best woman pilot.

There were other considerations. Several other women had preparations underway to make the flight and, from the publicity angle, George must have seen clearly that if another woman were to be first across the Atlantic, it would not help Amelia's career. There was one more factor: Amelia liked the idea of adventure.

In 1932, Amelia was voted "Outstanding American Woman of the Year," which she accepted on behalf of "all women." As her fame grew, she developed friendships with many people in high offices, most notably Eleanor Roosevelt, the First Lady from 1933-1945. Roosevelt shared many of Earhart's interests and passions, especially women's causes. After flying with Earhart, Roosevelt obtained a student permit, but did not pursue her plans to learn to fly.

Changing the Face of Women in Aviation

Flying the Atlantic solo put Amelia on the map as a celebrity woman and she began to enjoy financial success along with that territory. After the transatlantic flight, George Putnam maximized every opportunity and exploited every possibility of obtaining publicity for her. Although she never earned the enormous amounts of money credited to her by the newspapers, Amelia was in great demand on the lecture circuit and there were several career offers under consideration. Her immediate future was financially comfortable due to lecture fees and syndicated articles she wrote about the flight.

What George did for Amelia's career was threefold. First, he inspired and encouraged her; second, he worked on her behalf to publicize her name and reputation, creating openings for a financially viable career in aviation; and third, he introduced her to a wide circle of powerful people and obtained the necessary financial backing for her record-setting aviation attempts. She opened buildings, gave public speeches, and was interviewed and feted everywhere she went, possibly never realizing quite how much of the public's sustained interest was due to George's behind-the-scenes marketing.

Amelia's speeches always contained a firm but gentle reminder that women were the true equals of men. Whenever possible, Amelia flew to her engagements in order to publicize the practicality of aviation. Wherever she went, she passionately shared her stories, thus entertaining others to become passionate about their own lives.

During this period, Earhart became involved with The Ninety Nines, an organization of female pilots providing moral support and advancing the cause of women in aviation. Amelia was the organization's first elected president.

"I think it is just about the most important thing a girl can do, try her self out, do something."

Views on Marriage

Amelia married George Putnam in 1931. Earhart referred to her marriage as a "partnership" with "dual control." Just before the judge was due to arrive, Amelia handed George a letter. Among other things, she wrote:

"On our life together I want you to understand I shall not hold you to any medieval code of faithfulness to me, nor shall I consider myself bound to you similarly. If we can be honest, I think the difficulties which arise may best be avoided should you or I become interested deeply with anyone else. I must exact a cruel promise, and that is you will let me go in a year if we find no happiness together."

It is a most extraordinary testament. Few brides today, even given the relaxed conventions of modern times, would suggest to a bridegroom that sexual freedom for both parties was implicit in the marriage agreement. Earhart's ideas on marriage were liberal for the time, as she believed in equal responsibilities for both "breadwinners" and pointedly kept her own name rather than being referred to as Mrs. Putnam.

As much as she wanted the close companionship that she felt should be possible in marriage to George, she was not prepared to trade the former for the latter. She wanted both. George once said, "The idea that a woman's place is in the home is a lot of bunk." This statement of George's seemed to embody Amelia's entire approach to life: To put her entire concentration into whatever she was doing at the moment — work or play — and to enjoy it.

Honolulu to California

On January 11, 1935, Earhart became the first person to fly solo from Honolulu, Hawaii, to Oakland, California. Just three months later, Amelia again set a record, this time a double, by making the first successful solo flight from Los Angeles to Mexico City and then from Mexico City to Newark. In the long hours of these flights in 1935, Amelia began to form a plan. "There was one flight which I most wanted to attempt," she wrote. "A circumnavigation of the globe as near its waistline as could be."

Round-the-World Flight

Now approaching the age of forty, Amelia imagined this flight around the world would be the grand finale of her aviation career. After that there would be no major records left and her flying would simply be for pleasure, not for setting records. Beyond the expense of the aircraft, the costs for a 27,000-mile flight would be enormous.

Funding this mission was difficult. Purdue University came up with the idea of, and gave $80,000 for, "The Amelia Earhart Fund for Aeronautical Research." Its primary aim was to "develop scientific and engineering data of vital importance to the aviation industry." On July 24, 1936, on her thirty-ninth birthday, Amelia took possession of what would be her last airplane. She got the Purdue-funded Lockheed Electra 10E.

Even though she would be doing all the flying, Amelia realized she needed a well-trained navigator onboard. Amelia asked Harry Manning to fly with her on the most difficult leg of the trip, across the vast expanse of the Pacific. A second relief navigator, Fred Noonan, was also employed. In February 1937, Amelia was ready to publicly announce her plans.

Amelia's ambition to fly around the world would provide her with a major "first." She would be the first woman, if successful; but also, as she was later to confide to the President, her course was unique. Previous attempts always had been made to create time records and, therefore, the shortest possible route had been taken. Amelia decided to travel the longest possible distance by traversing the world at its waist, obviating the necessity to compete against existing records. Rather than finding the easy way, she sought the fullest challenge.

"Please know that I am aware of the hazards. I want to do it because I want to do it. Women must try to do things as men have tried. When they fail, their failure must be a challenge to others," Amelia said.

In March 1937, Amelia took-off from Oakland, California — thus, officially began her 'round-the-world flight — for Hawaii. The good-bye between her and George was public. However, the previous evening, she had told him: "I know that if I fail or if I am lost you will be blamed for allowing me to leave on this trip; the backers of the flight will be blamed and everyone connected with it. But it is my responsibility and mine alone." By taking responsibility for her life, she was taking a major step in trying to accomplish her dreams.

Flying along the equator from east to west, she made it to Hawaii in 15 hours and 47 minutes, a new speed record for that route. A few days later, though, after ground-looping during her takeoff from Hawaii for Howland Island, Amelia returned the plane to the Lockheed factory in California for repairs.

On May 21, 1937, Amelia again took off from California, this time for Florida. They flew over South America and Africa. Some of the goals of the 'round-the-world flight was to study the effects of high altitudes and extreme temperatures on aviation equipment and human stamina.

On June 1st, a small crowd assembled in Miami before dawn to watch Amelia and Fred set off for California, though this time they were heading west to east, reversing the planned direction for the flight around the world. By June 15th, they were in Karachi, Pakistan. In Southeast Asia, they got caught in a monsoon. On June 24th, Amelia and Fred prepared to depart for Australia's Port Darwin. She thought she would be back in Oakland no later than June 30th, but Amelia definitely hoped to be home for the Fourth of July. On July 2nd, they took off from Lae, New Guinea, with about twenty hours of fuel, to fly to Howland Island for a refueling stop. Somewhere along the journey home, however, the flight disappeared over the central Pacific Ocean near Howland Island.

Information about Amelia's and Fred's remaining hours has been pieced together by combining details from a variety of sources. The last reported radio transmission from her was at 8:45 a.m. on July 3rd. It was assumed her plane went down. Ships and planes scoured miles of the Pacific and its uninhabited islands. The official search for Amelia ended on July 19th, though her husband continued his private search until October. On January 5, 1939, Amelia Earhart was declared legally dead.

Paul Mantz was closely involved with Amelia in her record-breaking flights. He had been her co-pilot when she took part in the National Air Races. Paul believed that Amelia's plane had not been ready when she took-off on that fatal flight — he had anticipated at least another two day's work — and he was shocked to hear that she had gone without even saying good-bye to him.

Later, Paul's inquiries led him to believe that Amelia's husband, George Putnam, had pressured her into leaving early because he had organized a grand civic welcome for her return to Los Angeles, timed for the Fourth of July. If she delayed any longer leaving, and then allowing for contingency delays for weather conditions, spare parts, or engineering faults, she could not make it back in time. We will never know what happened to Amelia — except that she died doing what she loved...flying.

The Strides She Made

Fascination with Amelia Earhart's life, career, and disappearance continues to this day. She remains America's foremost female flier and her disappearance remains one of the great mysteries in aviation history.

Amelia Earhart was a well-known international celebrity during her lifetime. Her life is often cited as a motivational tale, especially for girls. Earhart is generally regarded as a feminist icon with her accomplishments in aviation inspiring a generation of female aviators, including more than 1,000 women pilots of the Women Air Force Service Pilots (WASP) who ferried military aircraft, towed gliders, flew target practice aircraft, and served as transport pilots during World War II.

Amelia Earhart became a symbol for women to take on more important roles during World War II, and today there are many female pilots serving the air forces throughout the world. Amelia Earhart was a pivotal figure who laid the foundation for women and men to take aviation a step further — a major step from atmospheric flight to spaceflight. She became a prelude to the achievements of Valentina Tereshkova, the first woman in space.

In addition to her achievements in aviation, Amelia Earhart is also remembered for championing equality between men and women, using aviation as a vehicle of similar pioneering spirit, in technical skills, and bravery. Many continued to protest that women had no place as pilots and that flying was the domain of men, but Amelia proved that this was not the case.

Amelia Earhart used her fame to speak out about women and society. "Wages should be based on work, not sex or any other consideration," she said. She married in 1931, but she did not accept the widespread view of marriage. "I believe that both men and women should be in the home some of the time and out some of the time. Fifty-fifty." She was ahead of her time.

She was a leading figure on the edge of society in the 1930s, blazing trails for a generation of women to follow. Although her own story ended much too quickly, the course that Amelia set in her life forged a path that gave women everywhere the chance to reach previously undreamed of goals.

Esther Morris

First Woman to Hold Political Office in the United States

- Born on August 8, 1814, in New York
- Orphaned by age ten
- In 1870, became the first woman to hold judicial office in the United States, thus, setting the stage for the 19th Amendment
- The State of Wyoming owes "Equality State" to Esther Morris
- Died in 1902

In 1869, Wyoming was the newest territory in the United States. Esther Morris fought for women's suffrage and helped secure the vote for women in Wyoming that year. It quickly became the first government in the United States to grant women the right to vote and to hold public office. The following year, Esther Morris became the first woman to hold a judicial position.

Esther Morris was a long-time advocate of equal rights. As a young woman she had dared to challenge pro-slavery agitators. As a widow she had fought for property rights of women. She ventured to the West when it was still an unsettled wilderness. And there she achieved national recognition as the first woman justice of the peace in the United States. Mrs. Morris was a woman of remarkable strength of mind.

Esther Morris fearlessly fought for women's rights throughout her lifetime. Life was not a bed of roses for her. She cultivated her skills as a young entrepreneur and earned her way as a business woman. Esther was a pioneer in many senses. Early on she realized that independence in her wallet bestowed her with a great deal of independence in her life. Hers is an example of a woman who juggled her busy career, motherhood, and marriage at the same time. Rather than foregoing one to accommodate the other, she proved to women of her time that it was alright to earn money, engage in political activism, and to be a mother and wife at the same time.

Family and Married life

The daughter of Daniel and Charlotte McQuigg, Esther Mae McQuigg was born August 8, 1814, near Spencer, Tioga County, New York. She was the eighth of eleven children in a family of comfortable means. After losing her parents, she became an orphan at age ten.

Esther showed entrepreneurial skills at an early age, when she apprenticed to a seamstress and ran a successful millinery business out of her grandparents' home, making hats, and buying and selling goods for women. In 1841, Esther McQuigg married Artemus Slack. She was twenty-seven years old. Just three years into the marriage, Mr. Slack died in a car accident and Esther sadly found herself a widow.

Esther moved to Peru, Illinois, to settle the property in her husband's estate. There, she realized the legal difficulties faced by women. She encountered legal roadblocks in settling her husband's affairs because women were not allowed to own or inherit property back then. During a long and difficult struggle to get possession of the land that was rightfully hers, she realized the injustice of property laws in relation to women. This was the first of many roadblocks that she experienced because of her gender. Esther was determined to do something to make a difference for all women. The widow resolved to devote as much of her time as possible to the betterment of such unfair conditions and to continue working for equal rights of women.

Anti-Slavery Worker

As a young, independent businesswoman, Esther joined the anti-slavery movement where she learned about many social injustices facing women under slavery. She was an ardent anti-slavery worker.

During an Abolition meeting at the Baptist church in Owego, New York, the pro-slavery element then predominant in the community became so intense that a prominent citizen asked the ladies to leave the church. He and the others who approved of slavery would tear down the building. Esther bravely stood up in her pew and addressed the meeting in a firm voice. "This church belongs to the Baptist people," she said. "No one has the right to destroy it. If it is proposed to burn it down, I will stay here and see who does it." Early on Esther demonstrated the character trait of fearlessly standing up to the truth. She became a voice for others who were afraid to stand up to themselves.

In 1841, Esther re-married, to John Morris, and they had two sons. Rather than give up her career to raise her children, Esther continued to perform her household dutifully as well as bring home money to raise her family comfortably. This was unusual at the time for a woman of her status since marriage and motherhood signaled household duties, nursing babies, and an end to a financially lucrative career.

The 1850 Illinois Census listed John Morris with real estate worth $2,000. Ten years later the census listed him as having no business and no real property. However, Esther Morris' real estate was valued at $4,000 and personal property at $1,000. John Morris was soon out of a job. Although Esther Morris earned money, she felt that it was important that her husband contribute financially, too. Esther Morris wanted her husband to find work.

Gold Fever in South Pass City

Like so many Americans, Esther and her new husband caught "gold fever" after the Civil War. They heard about the rich ore deposits in the mining camps of the Rocky Mountains. She thought of moving out West. She and her husband were ready to follow Horace Greeley's advice to "Go West, young man," so in 1869, they packed up their belongings and journeyed to South Pass City, the largest and most prosperous of the gold mining camps located high on the southeast of the Wyoming's Wind River Mountains. It was called Wyoming's "City of Gold."

Esther Morris wondered about her own future in the isolated gold camps of Wyoming. She did not know what awaited her. Like other women living in the Victorian age, she had experienced prejudice, discrimination, and unfair restrictions. While living in New York and Illinois, she had known women she considered just as intelligent and capable as their husbands, but their role in life was to serve as faithful wives and dedicated mothers. She had never neglected her husband or her sons, even though she was not overly fond of housekeeping. Esther would have preferred working outside the home, operating her own millinery shop. Sometimes, she became dissatisfied with mundane duties. Surely other wives felt restrained, too, longing to have more freedom. Women, she felt, should be recognized for their intelligence and abilities.

By 1869, no state or territory in the Unites States had ever given women the right to vote or to hold office. A few women of property had voted in New Jersey from 1776 to 1807. Other women had cast ballots in municipal and school elections, but these were isolated cases. Esther's mind was brewing with fresh ideas for making things better for women's enfranchisement. Her brother was cynical and quick to criticize her. When she left Illinois, he had issued her a challenge saying: "You will never live to see the day women vote."

Moving to Wyoming was out of Esther's comfort zone. There were more antelopes than people living in Wyoming at the time. Physically and emotionally, it was a daring move. It was Esther who gave courage to the male figures in her family to venture into the unknown. She became a crutch of courage for them.

During the peak of the gold mining boom, the time when Morris arrived in Wyoming, some 4,000 people lived in the three major gold camps of South Pass City. The dry, rocky landscape that confronted 55-year-old Morris as she stepped off the stage at South Pass City appeared startlingly different from the fertile landscape she had known in Illinois and New York. Her new home, at 7,500 feet in elevation, meant scratching out a living in a barren gulch at the mouth of a canyon. Occasional bushes along with a few lone trees tempered South Pass City's sharp-edged terrain. They moved there to open a saloon. Esther, however, would accomplish much more than that.

South Pass City was a difficult place to live in, especially during the harsh winters. Many saw the town ridden with problems and roadblocks of all sorts. South Pass area residents either left the camp for the winter or faced extreme isolation. Those who stayed on the mountain pass, like the Morrises, battled sub-zero temperatures, high winds, and deep snow that did not retreat until June. The high cost of transporting gold, a limited amount of the precious metal, insufficient water, and attacks by Indians were other reasons that so many left the area. Men outnumbered women four-to-one in this mountain community. It was not a safe area and was a gamble for Esther to settle her family there. Still, she would rather take the risk than stand still.

Instead, Esther saw the bleak landscape as one filled with opportunities. She knew this was the environment in which she would thrive and create a new life for herself and her family. It was in such a barren landscape that Esther Morris promoted her women's rights movement. The difficulties hardly stopped Esther from starting life anew and making new beginnings. Even though her husband was opposed to woman suffrage, Esther firmly believed in equal rights and so did her sons. Most importantly, South Pass City might offer a paying job for her husband.

"The women can do nothing without the help of the men. It is the rule of life that we must all work together."

South Pass City was a place that sprouted out of nearly nothing at the mention of the word "gold." The space around it was large and wide open. This was a good thing, for Mrs. Morris was a woman with wide open ideas that needed more room than she had in New York or Illinois.

Running for Office

Esther Morris was a woman of vision. Wyoming at that time had never even held a meeting of the territorial government. It was a brand new territory and Esther, with astonishing vision, saw that the women might find rights and opportunities there that were not available elsewhere in the country.

She thought a woman should be able to vote and hold office...the same as a man could.

Morris' past involvement in the anti-slavery and women's rights movement spurred her to suggest that the new territory of Wyoming could make world history by granting women the right to vote. Legalized women's suffrage would "prove a great advertisement," she felt, inducing more women and families to settle in Wyoming.

After she got herself settled in South Pass City, she paid a call on a man who had already argued hard for the same new and crazy sounding idea that she was bringing in from the East — Colonel William Bright. Though Bright thought women being able to vote and hold office made good sense, many opposed the idea.

Esther Morris held a tea party for her local delegate at the upcoming government meeting, with a proposal to allow women's suffrage, noting that if women were voting, they would vote pro-law and pro-government. The bill passed. The passage of this landmark suffrage law in 1869 helped make Wyoming famous as the "Equality State"... the first territory to enfranchise women. The clerk's telegraph to the world in part read:

"Wyoming, the youngest and one of the richest Territories in the United States, gave equal rights to women in actions as well as words."

Esther Morris was one of the 1,000 women in Wyoming who, on Friday, September 2, 1870, voted for the first time. It was time to prove women could hold office just as well.

However, on December 18, 1869, just eight days after the suffrage bill became law, James W. Stillman of South Pass City resigned his position as justice of the peace. Stillman, who had served as the magistrate since 1867, was adamant in his opposition to equal rights. He may have submitted his resignation of the public office in protest of the new law.

When Esther Morris learned Judge Stillman had resigned, she submitted her application for the office to the Sweetwater County Board of Commissioners. She was confident she could handle the duties of justice of peace since she had experience dealing with many different groups of people when she was in business in New York. In addition, it was time to step away from her cooking and gardening and do something that might help women coming along. Morris lobbied the twenty-two members of the territorial legislature — and became a judge.

While Esther's sons and some other citizens in the mining camp supported her, she did not have the support of her husband. This demanded more strength of character on her part to tread unknown territory with an unsupportive husband. Her sons, however, considered the suffrage law a milestone for Wyoming women. They admired and respected their mother for her alert mind, her mature judgment, her independent convictions, and the fact she did not make rash decisions. If she had the chance to be appointed or elected to a public office, they knew that she would faithfully perform her duties to the best of her ability.

On a gloomy day in February 1870, there arrived a package to Esther Morris. It contained the official document of the certificate of appointment. It was her commission as justice of the peace for Sweetwater County. The package was postmarked "Cheyenne, February 17, 1870." Esther opened it eagerly and read the letter:

"Madam: I have the honor to transmit herewith your commission as Justice of the Peace for the County of Sweetwater W.T. Should the same be accepted you will please take and subscribe the oath endorse thereon. ...I congratulate you upon holding the first Judicial position ever held by a woman. Please notify this office of your acceptance.

> *Very Respectfully*
> *Your Pub. Svt.*
> *Edwd. Lee*
> *Secretary and Acting Governor*
> *Wyoming Territory"*

Esther was grateful the decision had been made in her favor. On that February day in 1870, when Esther Morris walked from the family home along the north side of South Pass Avenue to the rented log courthouse where she would begin her duties as the new justice of the peace, she was wearing a black empress cloth dress underneath a heavy woolen coat. Esther had decided that since men who served as magistrates wore dark suits, black gowns were appropriate for a female judge.

Mrs. Morris had not expected to see many people in the courtroom that cold, winter day, but when she opened the pine door, she saw a gathering of bearded men, smoking cigars or pipes. They turned to stare at her. They would be judging her by the way she dealt with the defendants, their lawyers, and the decisions she made. The stately matron held her head high as she walked to the front of the room. In a strong voice, Mrs. Morris repeated the words of the oath, which her son read from a handwritten document:

"I, Esther Morris, do solemnly swear that I will support the Constitution of the United States, and the Organic Act of Wyoming and that I will

well and faithfully discharge the duties of the office upon which I am about to enter. So help me God."

The new judge had just sat down at the pine table when James Stillman and his attorney walked into the smoke-filled room. Having been arrested minutes before, the former justice of the peace had been brought to the courthouse to stand trial. Stillman had refused to hand over the docket and other public papers belonging to the office, probably because he opposed having a woman serve as a justice of the peace.

Since the former justice of the peace lived in South Pass City and was well known in the gold camp, townspeople discussed the unusual case at length. They were particularly interested since it would be a female magistrate who would be deciding Stillman's fate.

When court reconvened, there were even more people crowded into the log courtroom. Most of the shop owners on the avenue had closed their businesses so they could judge for themselves how the lady in black handled this unprecedented case.

The defense attorney stated that as the successor to the former justice of the peace, Judge Morris had a reason in demanding the docket to be returned to the court. Recognizing the defense attorney had made a key point, Judge Morris, without showing any emotion in her slightly wrinkled face, did not answer immediately.

When she applied for this position, Mrs. Morris had made up her mind that if appointed to the office, she would make every effort to be fair and just in all her decisions. Today, she was being tested. She dismissed the difficult case. With his head held high in the air, Stillman walked out of the courtroom, unescorted. Even though Esther advocated for the "elevation of women," she did not wish the "downfall of men." She cautioned women not to agitate.

The thirty or more cases Judge Morris handled from February 14, 1870, to November 1, 1870, were recorded. Esther Morris, as a working mother, held court over a camp of miners, gamblers, speculators, business owners, prostitutes, and robbers. Ten were assault cases and three were intent to kill. Most of her cases, however, were disagreements over debts. Judge Morris was paid $5.05 for the Stillman case, Case No.1. During her nine months as justice of the peace, Esther earned a total of $135.

Esther did not stop there. She fought for equal pay for men and women school teachers, the right for married women to own property, the right to serve on juries, and the right for women to hold office.

After Esther had completed the partial term on November 1, 1870, she was not nominated for another term. One of the founders of the Cheyenne newspaper, the *Wyoming Tribune*, stated: "The people of Sweetwater County had not had the good sense and judgment to nominate her for the ensuing term." James Stillman, the man whom Esther Morris was appointed to replace, was elected to be her successor as the magistrate in Sweetwater County.

"Mine was a test of woman's ability to hold office. And during it all, I do not know that I have neglected my family any more than ordinary shopping."

Esther Morris liked serving as justice of the peace. Her husband and her sons were working. Moving to South Pass City had been a wise decision for all the members of the family. She had made great advancement towards women's rights.

However, there were women who disagreed with the right for women to vote. They questioned whether the suffrage law, as well as the four other new laws beneficial to Wyoming women, would give them equality with their spouses. Many women may have had reservations about woman suffrage because they believed that it wasn't a "woman's place" to vote.

It was Wyoming's good fortune that Mrs. Morris, with her mature judgment and experience of middle age, had been selected for the trial run of women's suffrage. She cast the pattern for successful participation in politics by the women of the state and through it all she kept her sense of balance and humor.

One historian wrote: "…its (Wyoming) women were the first to be freed from the masculine tutelage of which law, religion, tradition, and custom bound them." Many "unfranchised" women, living in the states and territories, praised the example set by the little known territories in the West. Women waved banners and flags, while others sang as they marched in parades. Some women stood under lampposts displaying homemade signs, praising the men in the legislature and the governor of Wyoming for the foresight in giving women voting rights and the right to hold office."

Esther Morris took pride in what she had accomplished during her time as a public official. At the National Woman Suffrage Association Convention in Washington D.C. in 1871, Mrs. Amalia Post, wife of a banker in Cheyenne was the representative from Wyoming. Some 5,000 men and women were assembled in the hall when Mrs. Post read Esther Morris' letter. In many ways, it was a summary of woman suffrage in Wyoming.

"I have assisted in drawing a grand and petit jury, deposited a ballot, and helped canvas the votes after the election, and in performing all these duties I do not know as I have neglected my family any more than ordinary shopping, and I must admit that I have been better paid for the services rendered than for any I have ever performed. In some thirty civil actions, tried before me, there has been but one appeal taken, and the judgment was confirmed in the court above, and in criminal cases also before me there has been no call for a jury."

The same day on which Mrs. Post read Esther Morris' letter at the national convention, the following notice appeared in a Wyoming newspaper: "Female Suffrage bill has been defeated in the Dakota Legislature by a small majority. We wish Dakota women would all emigrate to Wyoming, where they would be appreciated."

Esther Morris gave credit to her family: "My family consists of a husband and three sons, all of whom have been more ready to assist me in the performance of my official duties than in my domestic affairs." Despite the lack of support by her husband, she stood by him in public rather than criticizing him.

Leaving Her Husband

Perhaps it was a case of cabin fever after being cooped up all season during a particularly bad winter of 1871-1872 that spurred Esther Morris to make some daring choices regarding her personal life. In 1871, less than a year after serving as justice of the peace, Mrs. Morris swore out a warrant for her husband's arrest on the charge of assault and battery. The record in the office of the Sweetwater County clerk stated: "Warrant issued, but not served. The matter being settled by the parties."

When John was elected coroner in 1872, Esther was hopeful this new responsibility would give him a new lease on life, but he continued to get into trouble with the law. Finally, in 1873, when domestic duties became almost impossible to solve because of his drinking problem and disagreeable disposition, she left him. John died in 1877.

Esther Morris traveled to Laramie, where she briefly lived with her son. The former judge remained unsettled however. She moved to Albany, New York, and then to Springfield, Illinois, where she spent her winters. Summers saw her returning to Wyoming, where she spent time with her sons. Morris' wandering ended in the 1880s when she returned to Cheyenne to live with her son.

Recognition for Woman Suffrage

During the statehood celebration in 1890, Esther was honored as a suffrage pioneer. In 1895, at the age of eighty, Esther Morris was a delegate to the Republican National Convention in Cleveland. The *Chicago Tribune* acknowledged her significance: "Her career is in some respects remarkable, especially as one of the early pioneers of Illinois and Wyoming… Few women of any period have been endowed with greater gifts than Esther Morris. Her originality, wit and rare powers of conversation would have given her a conspicuous position in any society."

Esther Morris died in Cheyenne on April 2, 1902, four months shy of her ninetieth birthday.

The Strides She Made

Life threw many challenges at Esther Morris, but nothing crushed her spirit. When she was ten, her parents died, leaving her an orphan. When her husband died, she was denied his property because she was a woman. Esther fought back each time.

As the first female in the nation ever to hold a judicial office, Esther realized that she was setting a precedent not only for the women of Wyoming, but for all the other women in the United States who had yet to be given the franchise. Esther Morris symbolized change for the American people. Her political stand set the precedent for greater achievements for female Supreme Court judges, secretaries of state, and potential female presidential candidates.

Suze Orman

World's No. 1 Personal Finance Expert

- Born on June 5, 1951, in Chicago
- World's No.1 Personal Finance Expert
- Emmy Award-winning television host, *New York Times* mega bestselling author, magazine and online columnist, writer, producer, and one of the top motivational speakers in the world

Suze Orman is America's most recognized expert on personal finance. She has taught people how to create money, how to save it, and invest it for the working class as well as the millionaire household. While there were many who knew how to save pennies here and there, it was a challenge to figure out how to save and invest for the larger picture. Suze Orman draws a connecting arrow between financial security and emotional happiness, between health and wealth, and between personal relationships and personal finance. Her television show, *The Suze Orman Show*, is a financial drug for millions of households in America.

Suze Orman is an Emmy Award-winning television host, *New York Times* mega bestselling author, magazine and online columnist, writer, producer, and one of the top motivational speakers in the world today. She has amassed a large following due to her own investment success and easy-to-follow financial strategies designed for average individuals. It all began in an epiphany that she had while waitressing at the Buttercup Bakery in California.

Birth and Family Background

Susan Lynn Orman was born June 5, 1951, in Chicago, Illinois, to parents of Russian Jewish heritage. In her youth, Suze had difficulty forming words, leading to challenges with reading and writing. She had a speech impediment and could not pronounce her Rs, Ss, or Ts properly, so words such as "beautiful," for example, came out as "boobital."

When Suze was a child, her working class family struggled financially. In grammar school, Suze habitually scored among the lowest in reading exams. She was not an "A" student by any means. In her family, however, going to college was not an option. She knew she would have to earn her way through college and would have to attend a community college or a state school. She applied to the University of Illinois at Urbana-Champaign and was accepted. She worked as a dishwasher in the campus cafeteria to help pay her bills. Part way through her college career, she left to see America, with just $300 in her pocket.

The money soon ran out and Suze needed work. She applied for a job as a waitress at the Buttercup Bakery, a great little place where she used to get coffee. Suze was thrilled to get a job. She earned a bachelor's degree in social work at the University of Illinois at the age of thirty, but was still a waitress, making $400 a month.

Now, Suze was an official college graduate, working as a waitress. She stayed at the Buttercup Bakery and dreamt of opening her own restaurant. Her official start in financial investing did not begin until she was thirty.

"In all realms of life, it takes courage to stretch your limits, express your power, and fulfill your potential. It's no different in the financial realm."

One day, Orman began to dream of nicer things, of doing better than a waitress. She dreamt big, but her dreams required seed money, of which she had none. No one makes it alone. Fred Hasbrook, a friend at the bakery, gathered $20,000 between himself and some friends. The final total was $50,000. It was attached with a note that read: "This is for people like you, so that your dreams can come true. To be paid back in ten years if you can, with no interest." Fred Hasbrook had become her guardian angel in disguise, the one who would make or break her dream. We all have a guardian angel that watches out for us when we are in need. For Suze Orman, Fred Hasbrook was one of them. "People first, then money, then things," said Orman.

Suze Orman Gets Ripped Off

Suze Orman knew nothing about financial investing when she was thirty. She sought help from a representative at Merrill Lynch. She met with a broker, and put her money into an account there. Although she had told him that she only made $400 a week and needed to keep her money safe, the broker chose to pursue the risky strategy of buying options. He told her that she could make "a quick $100 a week." The plan worked well at first, but she ended up losing all of her money within three months.

"A big part of financial freedom is having your heart and mind free from worry about the what-ifs of life."

Suze Orman read the *Wall Street Journal* and *Barron's*, and she tuned in to the PBS financial series *Wall Street Week*. She had neither a Master's in business administration nor a background in money management. The knowledge she acquired was self-taught. Meanwhile, Orman had been trying to learn as much about investing as she could.

After losing all her money, Orman decided to become a broker and applied to the same Merrill Lynch office where she had lost her earlier investment. She used her pain to make a difference in the lives of others. In 1983, she left to join another firm, becoming Vice President of Investments at Prudential Bache Securities. Four years later, in 1987, Suze Orman opened her own firm, The Suze Orman Financial Group, and resigned from Prudential. She acted as the Director of the firm until 1997 when she decided to focus more on her writing and speaking career.

Health and Wealth

One of Orman's mantras is the intrinsic connection between health and wealth. The more debt you have, the more depressed you become, the more weight you gain, and other health problems arise. Achieving financial success is, according to Ms. Orman, a way to lead a healthy life. With her books, television show, and other media efforts, Suze Orman has established herself as one of the top personal financial experts in the United States.

"My job is to be the financial truth crusader. Hope for the best, but plan for the worst."

Money or Your Life

Orman got her first media exposure through a local radio station after writing to complain about another guest that provided incorrect information on an investment product. "The next Saturday I went down there and did a show. After that, my phone started to ring off the hook," Orman told *Success* magazine. Soon Orman became a guest expert for other radio and television programs.

Planning for the future — 20, 30, 40 years down the road — is her signature. She helps people to decide whether or not they can afford goods and services, from buying a $55 wristwatch to a $250,000 sailboat. Orman shows true human nature when it comes to money. Love changes, family dynamics change, and friends change when money gets involved. Be ready for it. She has counseled:

"After you marry, every asset either of you acquires is jointly held. That's why you both need to be in sync on your long-term financial goals, from paying off the mortgage to putting away for retirement. Ideally, you should talk about all this before you wed. If you don't, you can end up deeply frustrated and financially spent."

In July 2009, *Forbes* magazine named Orman eighteenth on their list of "The Most Influential Women In Media." In May 2008 and 2009, *Time Magazine* named Orman as one of the "TIME 100, The World's Most Influential People." In April 2008, Orman was presented with the Amelia Earhart Award for her message of financial empowerment for women.

Suze Orman analyzes what makes individuals spend and save, and all of the psychological factors that are involved with money. She dissects them, sheds light on them, and helps Americans and people worldwide gain financial freedom. Her most notable books include *The 9 Steps to Financial Freedom*, *The Courage to Be Rich*, and *The Road to Wealth*.

"Owning a home is a keystone of wealth, both financial affluence and emotional security."

After her publishing success, Orman began hosting a weekly television show on CNBC titled *The Suze Orman Show*. She has won two Emmy Awards for her PBS pledge drives and has appeared on numerous different talk shows to discuss financial matters. In 2007, *Business Week* named Orman one of the top ten motivational speakers in the world. She was the only woman on that list, thereby making her 2007's top female motivational speaker in the world.

The Strides She Made

Suze Orman exposed topics on educational aid, retirement planning, and long-term investment vehicles in a lay person's language. She defined a "revocable trust" in easy-to-understand terms rather than making it seem difficult. She explained clearly how a "revocable trust" would improve their quality of life and could make all the difference in a person's financial health.

Orman has introduced several methods to help individuals pay off their bills and enjoy the money they have left over while investing and saving for the future. As a result, thousands of individuals have been able to get out of debt and live a more enjoyable life without the overhanging debt and stress that accompanies it.

At the time of this writing, Suze Orman is more vibrant than ever, empowering men, women, and children alike with her financial advice. She urges her followers to plan for a long life, ninety years or more, and to make sure that they have good retirement plans.

Emmeline Pankhurst

Leader of the British Suffragette Movement

- Born on July 14th, 1858, in Manchester, England
- British political activist and leader of the British suffragette movement, which helped women win the right to vote
- In 1878, she married Richard Pankhurst, a barrister twenty-four years her senior known for supporting a woman's right to vote
- Died on June 14, 1928

Emmeline Pankhurst (born Emmeline Goulden) was a British political activist and leader of the British suffragette movement, which helped women win the right to vote. Pankhurst founded the Women's Social and Political Union (WSPU), an all-women suffrage advocacy organization. The group quickly became infamous when its members smashed windows and assaulted police officers. Pankhurst, her daughters, and other WSPU activists were sentenced to repeated prison sentences, where they staged hunger strikes to secure better conditions.

Emmeline Pankhurst devoted her whole being to politics, often at the expense of a personal existence. A doer rather than a thinker, Pankhurst was involved in a range of issues on several fronts: as Poor Law Guardian, as a member of the Manchester School Board, and with local politics.

Birth and Background

Emmeline Goulden was born July 15, 1858, in a Manchester suburb in England. The family into which she was born had been steeped in political agitation for generations. She was trained by her father to read the newspaper while he ate breakfast. Her brothers called her "the dictionary" for her faultless spelling. She learned the piano with equal facility, as a tiny child she played the piano at sight and she never practiced. Her good ear in music would translate into her political life in her later years.

Her father Robert Goulden gained public applause as the foremost amateur actor in theater-loving Manchester. He owned a theater in Salford for several years, where he played the leads in several plays by William Shakespeare. Pankhurst absorbed an appreciation of drama and theatrics from her father, which she used later in social activism. Her mother was a good cook, her kitchen producing enormous quantities of pickles, jams, and pies. There was much entertaining around their home.

Although their first son died at the age of two, Pankhurst's parents had ten other children; she was the eldest of five daughters. The position of the eldest sister in so large a family was often strained with great responsibilities. Emmeline was forced to mature early, leaving pranks to her youngsters.

One night she lay in bed, pretending to be asleep. It was a custom of her father and mother to make the round of the bedrooms every night before they themselves went to bed. When her parents entered the room one night, her father bent over her, gazed down at her, and said, "What a pity she wasn't born a lad."

"The education of the English boy, then as now, was considered a much more serious matter than the education of the English boy's sister. My parents, especially my father, discussed the question of my brother's education as a matter of real importance. My education and that of my sister were scarcely discussed at all."

Family Background in Politics

Emmeline Pankhurst's father came from a modest Manchester merchant family with its own background of political activity. Robert Goulden was active in local politics and served for several years on the Salford Town Council. He was also against slavery. Her father was prominent enough in the movement to be appointed on a committee to meet and welcome Henry Ward Beecher when he arrived in England for a lecture tour. His mother worked with the Anti-Corn Law League. Her father was also an enthusiastic supporter of dramatic organizations including the Manchester Athenaeum and the Dramatic Reading Society.

Emmeline's young mind was early disposed to rebellion and reform by the stories of her paternal grandfather, who, as a youth, had been kidnapped by the "Press Gang" for service in the Navy abroad. Pankhurst's paternal grandfather was present at the Peterloo Massacre when cavalry charged and broke up a crowd demanding parliamentary reform.

Social Context of Britain

Manchester was then the center of the women's emancipation movement. It was a time of heart-stirring struggles for constitutional liberty and the freedom of the human mind and personality, both in England and abroad. In all these Robert Goulden was on the side of liberation.

Harriet Beecher Stowe's novel in defense of the slaves, *Uncle Tom's Cabin*, dominated the Goulden household. The mother made it a frequent subject of discussion and story for her children. She was enthusiastic in fundraising activities to aid the newly emancipated slaves, and little Emmeline was given a "lucky bag" to collect pennies for the cause.

When she was about fourteen, the future militant first attended a meeting in support of the cause she was to make her own. Returning from school as her mother set out to hear the famous suffrage advocate Lydia Becker, Emmeline begged to be taken too, and went with her mother.

A French Education

In 1872, when Emmeline was fourteen years old, her father took her to France. She was placed in a prestigious school there. Her roommate was Noemie Rochefort, daughter of the great republican, communist, journalist, and swordsman, Henri Rochefort. The school was one of the pioneer institutions for the higher education of girls. Whilst their brothers were being prepared for the family business, or some other, the girls were expected to stay at home, dusting the drawing room and arrange flowers. At eighteen, she returned home and took her place in her father's home as a finished young lady.

Marriage to Dr. Pankhurst

Dr. Pankhurst was leading the peace party in Manchester. It was he who induced the north-country Liberal Associations to demand Gladstone's return to the Liberal leadership "to save the peace of Europe." Emmeline and her parents attended a great meeting he was to address.

On the initiative of Dr. Pankhurst, a tremendous campaign was made to get women's names on the Register. Dr. Pankhurst drafted a Bill to secure votes for women on the same terms as men, but it did not pass.

Emmeline Pankhurst sympathized with and worked for the woman suffrage movement and came to know Dr. Pankhurst, whose work for woman suffrage had never ceased. It was Dr. Pankhurstt who drafted the first enfranchisement bill, known as the Women's Disabilities Removal Bill and introduced into the House of Commons in 1870 by Jacob Bright. Dr. Pankhurst acted as counsel for the Manchester women, who tried in 1868 to be placed on the register as voters. He also drafted the bill giving married women absolute control over their property and earnings, a bill which became a law in 1882.

Emmeline and Dr. Pankhurst married in 1879.

Her Political Thinking

Her parents had encouraged their young daughter to be aware of injustice, and Emmeline was involved in social reform all her life. Her commitment to democracy and to women's emancipation remained an essential part of her political identity. For Emmeline the women's vote was only ever a means to an end.

Emmeline criticized trade unions for their socialist ideals. Unions, she insisted, had tried to prevent women from entering previously masculine trades. Consequently, they were condemned for being anti-feminist.

"There can be no real peace in the world until women, the mother half of the human family, is given liberty in the councils of the world."

Life with Dr. Pankhurst

Dr. Pankhurst lent the weight of his honored name to the suffrage movement in the trials of its struggling youth. He worked all his life to organize, educate, and prepare for the revolt that was one day to come. Unquestionably, this pioneer man suffered in popularity for his feminist views. He also suffered financially and politically, yet he never wavered.

About a year after their marriage, Emmeline's daughter Christabel was born; eighteen months later, her second daughter Sylvia came. Two other children followed, and for some years she was immersed in domestic affairs. However, she never lost interest in community affairs. Emmeline Pankhurst had a total of five children.

Dr. Pankhurst did not desire that Emmeline should turn herself into a household machine. It was his firm belief that society as well as the family stands in need of women's services. While the children were infants, she was serving on the executive committee of the Women's Suffrage Society and also on the executive board of the committee, which was working to secure the Married Women's Property Act. This act passed in 1882.

In 1883, Dr. Pankhurst resigned from the Liberal Association and announced his intention of running as an independent Parliamentary candidate at the next general election. Dr. Pankhurst's election address was probably one of the most challenging ever offered to a British constituency; it included from the British constitution of "all non-representative element," covering the abolition of the Monarchy and the House of Lords, adult suffrage for both sexes, the disestablishment and disendowment of the Church and removal of religious privileges and disabilities, free compulsory secular education, nationalization of the land, an international tribunal, drastic naval and military reductions, and finally Home Rule for Ireland, for which no English candidate had yet dared to take a stand.

In a poll, there were 6,000 supporters for Dr. Pankhurst and 18,000 for his opponent. From the distress of it, his health failed. Financial difficulties grew up from which he never recovered. Emmeline's husband lost many professional clients and they were financially bankrupt.

Money Becomes Tight

With Dr. Pankhurst's reputation failing and money becoming tight, Emmeline Pankhurst made a conscious decision to shoulder the financial weight in order to provide for her family. She disliked having to be dependent on others in order to ease responsibilities from her shoulder. Her taste for freedom was far greater.

Mrs. Pankhurst, eager for financial independence, determined to be a shopkeeper, dreaming in her ardent fashion that she would emancipate her husband from professional work to concentrate on politics. She and her sister Mary opened shop as Emerson & Co. with a miscellaneous array of fancy goods and, in 1891, she became affiliated with the Women's Franchise League.

Losing a Son

Dr. Pankhurst changed his work routine and started commuting to Manchester. Mrs. Pankhurst frequently accompanied him. During her absence, their four-year-old son, Frank, suddenly took ill. The child died without the appropriate treatment. Her loss aroused in Mrs. Pankhurst a bitter revolt against poverty and its hardships. Had she not chosen that dismal neighborhood, she told herself, her boy would not have been lost; the doctors would have treated him very differently had she gone to them, not as a little shopkeeper but as the wife of a distinguished lawyer.

The death of her son had a profound impact on Emmeline. She also became aware of how differently people with financial prosperity were treated from the people who lacked it.

Injustices to Women

Emmeline noticed the injustices taking place in England at the time. She saw the stigma of pauperism being applied to workhouse children. If they are treated like paupers, of course they will grow to be paupers, later becoming permanent burdens on society. However, if they are regarded as children under the guardianship of the state, they would turn out to be different and, thus, be less of a burden. She realized that the vote in women's hands was not just a right, but also a desperate necessity to bring about change.

Emmeline also witnessed many of the tragedies affecting women at the time. Aging women over sixty and seventy years old did physical work, sewing, and most of the things that kept the house clean and which supplied the inmates with clothing. The aging men were different. One could not get very much work out of them. Very little was done by the aging man in terms of work. Men were talkers while women were workers.

Many of them were widows of skilled artisans who had pensions from their unions, but the pensions had died with the men. These women, who had given up the power to work for themselves and had devoted themselves to working for their husbands and children, were left penniless. There was nothing for them to do, but to go into the workhouse. Many of them were widows of men who had served their country in the army or navy.

The Death of her Husband

In 1898, Dr. Pankhurst died. His death occurred suddenly and left Emmeline with the heavy responsibility of caring for a family of children. She was married for nineteen years.

Despite her other responsibilities as a women's activist leader, Emmeline did not ignore her private duties as a mother, however inadequately she performed them. Emmeline was always very possessive of her daughters, even when they were grown-up women.

Political Activism Work

Emmeline Pankhurst was convinced that if civilization is to advance at all in the future, it must be through the help of women — women freed of their political shackles, women with full power to work their will in society.

In 1900, Emmeline was asked to stand as a candidate for the Manchester School Board. She found that in the school system also, men had all the advantages. Male teachers received much higher salaries than the women. Furthermore, women teachers received no extra pay for their extra work. In spite of this added burden, Emmeline found that the women cared a great deal more about the children than the men.

There was one winter when there was a great deal of poverty in Manchester. The female teachers were spending their slender salaries to provide regular dinners for destitute children and were giving up their time to waiting on them and seeing that they were nourished. "We have to feed them before we can teach them," the women said.

In 1902, Susan B. Anthony paid a visit to Manchester and that visit was one of the contributory causes that led to the founding of the militant suffrage organization, the Women's Social and Political Union. "The militancy of women has harmed no human life save the lives of those who fought the battle of righteousness. Time alone will reveal what reward will be allotted to the women," said Pankhurst.

After spending some time touring the American lecture circuits, proclaiming the evils of Bolshevism, Emmeline Pankhurst embarked on her third career: promoter of social purity. It was here that her formidable talents and beliefs bore fruit: her public speaking, her organizational skills, her commitment to social purity, and her feminism were all used to striking effect.

Destruction of Property and Prison Sentences

The Women's Revolution was in full swing by November 1911. Emmeline announced her intentions of leading her followers to destroy public and private property on a large scale, for which she was imprisoned for two months. More window-smashing continued. These events of early March 1912, and of Emmeline's role as leader of the demonstrations, received widespread condemnation in the press. Emmeline was both a convicted offender serving a two months' prison sentence and a prisoner on remand waiting to be charged with a more serious offense. She was in poor health with bronchitis. Emmeline's petition for release on bail so that she could recover her health and prepare her case was refused. After serving her time in prison, she was released.

*"Women become the nurturing mothers of men, their sisters
and uncomplaining helpmates."*

After spending much of her life fighting for women's rights, Emmeline Pankhurst died June 14, 1928.

The Strides She Made

Her voice spoke mostly to a younger generation, offering them not just the vote but a new freedom that their parents could never have envisaged. By defying the gender, class, and cultural assumptions that underpinned the British establishment, she became the radical symbol of that political age. Emmeline Pankhurst's political legacy lives on more significantly in her contribution to widening the base of British Parliamentary democracy.

She believed passionately that women's suffrage was the only realistic way to deliver social justice for women and to build a truly democratic Britain.

Eleanor Roosevelt

First Lady of the U.S and First Lady of the World

Eleanor Roosevelt lit people's faces wherever she went. She visited coal miners, veterans, and sharecroppers. No first lady had ever done that before.

- Born on October 11, 1884, in New York City
- Spent twelve years as the First Lady of the United States
- Chairperson for the UN Commission on Human Rights
- Died in 1962

"*You* can never really live anyone else's life. The influence you exert is through your own life and what you've become yourself." Eleanor Roosevelt lived her own life, setting new trends as a first lady and doing acts of kindness on her own merit. She spent twelve years as the First Lady of the United States. As the First Lady, she refused to remain in the shadow of her husband, President Roosevelt, and stepped forward to be in his light. She was appointed the UN chair of the Commission on Human Rights. She ranks among the best known and most influential women in American history.

Birth and Family Life

Anna Eleanor Roosevelt was born on October 11, 1884, in New York City. Her parents were Elliott and Anna Hall Roosevelt. Her father suffered from physical problems and alcoholism and he was frequently in and out of sanitariums. Young Eleanor worshipped her father, despite his shortcomings. Eleanor's father made her feel important and loved, but he drank a lot and wasn't home much. Eleanor's mother made her feel less beautiful. She thought Eleanor was too serious. She called Eleanor "Granny" in front of people. Anna Hall was troubled by her daughter's lack of beauty. She tried hard to bring Eleanor up well so that her manners would compensate for her looks, but her mother's efforts only made her more keenly conscious of her shortcomings, her plain looks, and lack of manners. This lonely girl, however, would grow up to write books and magazine articles, give speeches to large audiences, meet with leaders of many nations, and donate her time to countless causes and organizations.

Attention and admiration were two things Eleanor craved in her childhood. She was made to feel that nothing about her would attract attention or would bring her admiration. At age six, Eleanor was sent to a convent school. One day, one of the girls at the convent swallowed a penny. Every attention was given to that girl. Eleanor wanted to be that center of interest, so she went to one of the sisters and told her that she, too, had swallowed a penny. Evidently the story was not true. The nun called for her mother, who took Eleanor away in disgrace. This habit of lying stayed with Eleanor for years. It was only later on in her life that she realized there was nothing to fear.

In 1892, when Eleanor was eight years old, her mother died of diptheria. Less than a year later, her younger brother died. Eleanor's mother had left her grandmother as guardian of her children. Eleanor's father had no wife, no children, and no hope.

Eleanor always felt close to her father, even though she no longer lived with him. She says in her autobiography: "There started that day a feeling which never left me, that he and I were very close and someday would have a life of our own together. He told me to write to him often, to be a good girl, not to give any trouble, to study hard, to grow up into a woman he could be proud of, and he would come to see me whenever possible" (*This is My Story*, p. 10). On August 14, 1894, just before Eleanor was ten years old, word came that her father had died. Her grandmother thought it best that Eleanor not go to the funeral.

Marriage to Franklin Roosevelt

Eleanor Roosevelt described herself as "a solemn child, without beauty, entirely lacking in the spontaneous joy and mirth of youth." In 1900, her uncle, Theodore Roosevelt, was elected President of the United States.

When Eleanor was fifteen years old, she was sent to school in England, as girls from rich families often were. Her teacher encouraged Eleanor to read and think for herself, to find important things to do, and to speak up for what she believed in.

Eleanor Roosevelt returned to New York when she was eighteen and fell in love with a rich, distant cousin named Franklin Delano Roosevelt, a student at Harvard University. They were married on March 17, 1905. Eleanor had a very domineering mother-in-law named Sara, who told Eleanor what clothes to buy and what food to serve. When Eleanor's children were born, Sara told her how to raise them. She built Eleanor and Franklin a house next to hers, with connecting doors on all floors. Her mother-in-law even chose their furniture.

In 1911, Franklin was elected to the New York State Senate. Eleanor was glad to move to Albany, especially since Sara didn't live there. In 1920, Democratic presidential nominee James Cox chose Franklin to be his running mate. In 1932, Franklin became president, leading to his and Eleanor living and working in the White House for the next twelve years. As First Lady, Eleanor held the first press conference and traveled throughout the country, reporting back to Franklin on the concerns of Americans. Eleanor also gave lectures, spoke at colleges, visited factories, and got involved in social relief programs.

War Efforts

World War I was a time of despair and chaos. Lots of dark things were happening; many, under the radar. "It is better to light a candle than curse the darkness," said Eleanor of that time.

From early morning to midnight, Eleanor organized women to knit warm clothes for sailors. In naval hospitals, she saw men too wounded to ever go home. Some were shell-shocked and locked behind bars. They had no one to talk to and nothing to do all day. Eleanor was outraged. This time, she didn't keep quiet — she hounded public officials until these men got the best care.

"A woman is like a tea bag: you can't tell how strong she is until you put her in hot water."

During the Great Depression, Franklin sent Eleanor around the country to talk to Americans. Rather than complain about them, Eleanor lit people's faces wherever she went. She visited coal miners, veterans, and sharecroppers. No first lady had ever done that. She told Franklin what she saw and what she thought needed to be done.

Eleanor joined the board of the League of Women Voters. Women had just won the right to vote, and Eleanor saw the organization as a way to remain politically involved outside of her husband's career. She also worked as co-director of the Democratic Party's National Women's Committee.

Apart from her social service, Eleanor was busy raising five children. She never put her duties as a mother on the back-burner, despite her busy work schedule. As the first lady, she did not have to overwhelm her life with social work. She could have chosen an easier path, filled with gala dinners, fancy gowns, media glamour, and plenty of free time. Yet, she never picked the easy path. She wanted to make a difference when given the opportunity.

World War 1 ended in 1918. Two years later, Franklin came down with polio. The doctors said he would never walk again. Sara said Franklin must stop working and move back to the family home. Eleanor knew Franklin dreamed of holding public office and that she had to help him realize his dream. Sara was furious with her and tried to turn Eleanor's children against her. Eleanor held firm.

Franklin slowly recovered. Eleanor started making speeches, talking on the radio, and writing magazine articles. She reminded women, who had recently won the right to vote, that they had important things to do. She said that "women must get into politics and stay in."

"The most important thing in any relationship is not what you get, but what you give."

The most important thing in any relationship is not what you get, but what you give.

In 1941, America was at war again. During World War II, Eleanor became one of the country's most effective and tireless morale builders, visiting allied nations and offering motherly comfort to wounded soldiers in military hospitals. Franklin sent Eleanor across both oceans. She traveled thousands of miles and met over 400,000 men and women. She toured many hospital wards, stopping at every sick bed. All through Franklin's presidency Eleanor spoke up for what she believed in and she insisted that all Americans deserved decent housing, health care, and education. She spoke out against racism, anti-Semitism, and the internment of Japanese Americans during World War II. She said:

"I have never felt that anything really mattered but knowing that you stood for the things in which you believed and had done the very best you could."

Some Americans disliked what Eleanor said and what she believed in. They mocked her. They called her "ugly" and a "do-gooder." No matter what they said, though, Eleanor refused to keep quiet and continued to pursue her activism work. By and large, however, she was dearly loved by Americans. Observed Eleanor:

"It is not unusual to find that women in particular are criticized for what they do. Do what you feel in your heart to be right for you'll be criticized anyway. You'll be damned if you do, and damned if you don't."

Joining the United Nations

After Franklin's death in 1945, President Harry Truman appointed Eleanor Roosevelt to the United Nations. She headed a committee of people from different countries. After two years, the committee agreed on a declaration of rights for people all over the world.

Eleanor Roosevelt became the chairperson for the Commission on Human Rights, where she sponsored a Universal Declaration of Human Rights. In 1948, the United Nations adopted the Universal Declaration of Human Rights, which outlines the rights of all people to freedom from slavery and torture, and freedom of movement, speech, religion, and assembly, as well as rights of all people to social security, work, health, housing, education, culture, and citizenship. Further, it states that all people have the equal right to all these human rights "without distinction of any kind such as race, color, sex, language, or other status."

"Great minds discuss ideas; average minds discuss events; small minds discuss people."

The girl who felt unloved, feared people, lacked self-esteem, and felt homely about herself blossomed into a self-confident woman who created the trend for first ladies to get out there and do something meaningful — not to just host gala parties and live in the shadow of their husbands. Eleanor Roosevelt maintained an active political and social life right up until her death in 1962. She was seventy-eight years old.

The Strides She Made

Eleanor Roosevelt became a ray of hope for millions of women around the world. She allowed no one to keep her down because of her lack of beauty. Instead, she rose above them because she felt beautiful inside of herself. She believed in herself, saying: "One can, even without any particular gifts, overcome obstacles that seem insurmountable if one is willing to face the fact that they must be overcome; that, in spite of timidity and fear, in spite of a lack of special talents, one can find a way to live widely and fully."

Wilma Rudolph

First American Woman to Win Three Gold Medals at the Olympics

It was at the tender age of five that Wilma Rudolph contracted polio. Yet, at the Summer Olympics of 1960, she won a gold medal in the 100 meter dash, the 200 meter dash, and the 400 meter relay race.

- Born in 1940 in Clarksville, Tennessee
- Contracted polio at age five and was told she would never be able to walk again
- First woman to win three Olympic Gold medals at the Olympics in 1960
- Civil rights and women's rights pioneer
- Died on November 12, 1994

*I*t was at the tender age of five that Wilma Rudolph contracted polio. Yet, at the Summer Olympics of 1960, she won a gold medal in the 100 meter dash, a gold medal in the 200 meter dash, and a gold medal in the 400 meter relay race. At age twenty, Wilma Rudolph became the first American woman to win three gold medals at a single Olympics. Wilma Rudolph, once known as the sickliest child in Clarksville, had become the fastest woman in the world. It all became possible because of one character trait: she believed in herself.

Birth and Family Background

Weighing just over four pounds at birth in 1940, it was a miracle that Wilma Rudolph ever made it beyond her first birthday, but she did. She came from a family of twenty-two children. As a child, she was very sickly. Her mother always nursed her at home. Doctors were a luxury for the Rudolph family and were not easy to access. Only one doctor in Clarksville, Tennessee, treated people of color and that is the one Wilma Rudolph was taken to see.

At the age of five, Wilma Rudolph contracted polio. In those days, most children who got polio either died or were permanently crippled. Polio was the world's most dreaded disease at that time — a cure for it was not found until 1955. The news spread around Clarksville: Wilma would never walk again. It was a sad predicament for the Rudolph family.

Fighting Polio

Doctors and nurses at the hospital helped Wilma do exercises to make her paralyzed leg stronger. At home, Wilma practiced her legs constantly, even when it hurt; this was the sole focus of her childhood — her legs. While other children her age ran and played outside, Wilma concentrated on her legs. To Wilma, what hurt most was that the local school would not let her attend because she could not walk. Now, any other child's self-esteem and self-worth would have been crushed for being denied school, but not Wilma's. Even as a little girl, she never allowed the society around her to crush her inner spirit. Tired of crying all the time, she decided to fight back. Wilma worked so hard at her exercises that the doctors decided she was ready for a heavy steel brace. With the brace supporting her leg, she didn't have to hop anymore. School was possible at last, and Wilma was excited to be able to go to school.

School, however, was not what she thought it would be. It was an unhappy place for Wilma, not the fun-loving place that she had anticipated. Her classmates made fun of her brace. While other children played basketball, Wilma had to watch from the sidelines. They laughed at her. Wilma fought the sadness by doing more leg exercises. Her family always cheered her on. Wilma picked up every stone that was thrown at her and was quietly building a foundation with them. People tried to keep her down as a cripple who would never walk again, but Wilma fought back.

"I believe in me more than anything in this world."

A devout Christian, Wilma always felt safest in church. One day, during mass, she took the brave step of removing her brace and walking into the church. Everyone looked, wide-eyed. Wilma practiced walking as often as she could after that. When she was twelve, she was able to take off the brace for good. "My doctor told me I would never walk again. My mother told me I would... and I believed my mother," she said.

A coach spotted Wilma at a basketball court during a high school game and thought she would make a good runner. A full athletic scholarship enabled her to enter Tennessee State University, the first member of her family to go to college. "When the sun is shining, I can do anything; no mountain is too high, no trouble too difficult to overcome," she said.

Wilma trained and improved everyday as a runner. It was an exhilarating experience for her and she fell in love with herself while doing it. Running enhanced her sense of self-worth, it proved that she was capable of anything in life if she set her mind to it, and it made her more determined than ever to be successful. She said of running: "I ran and ran and ran every day, and I acquired this sense of determination, this sense of spirit that I would never, never give up, no matter what else happened."

"I loved the feeling of freedom in running, the fresh air, the feeling that the only person I'm competing with is me."

Olympic Champion

Eight years after she mailed her brace away, Wilma's long legs and years of hard work carried her to the Summer Olympics of 1960. She won a gold medal in the 100 meter dash, a gold medal in the 200 meter dash, and a gold medal in the 400 meter relay race. Rudolph became an international star, in part because it was the first year that the Olympics had received international, widespread television coverage. Rudulph said:

"Winning is great, sure, but if you are really going to do something in life, the secret is learning how to lose. Nobody goes undefeated all the time. If you can pick up after a crushing defeat and go on to win again, you are going to be a champion someday."

Wilma Rudolph, once known as the sickliest child in Clarksville, had become the fastest woman in the world. Her triumphs were not possible without the struggle. "Believe me, the reward is not so great without the struggle," she said.

Rudolph was the United Press Athlete of the Year 1960 and Associated Press Woman Athlete of the Year for 1960 and 1961. Also in 1961, the year her father died, Rudolph won the James E. Sullivan Award, an award for the top amateur athlete in the United States, and got to visit with President John F. Kennedy.

Wilma never forgot the people who helped her achieve her unimaginable success. It was not a journey she did alone. Her mother encouraged her, people in her church cheered for her, and her coach inspired her. Some people helped her while others tried to crush her. Wilma kept her head high and embraced the vision of her believers.

"No matter what accomplishments you make, somebody helps you."

At age twenty, Wilma Rudolph became the first American woman to win three gold medals at a single Olympics. The story of all she overcame to win at the Olympics was especially inspiring to women. "It doesn't matter what you're trying to accomplish. It's all a matter of discipline. I was determined to discover what life held for me beyond the inner city streets," Wilma said.

Wilma Rudulph died on November 12, 1994, in Brentwood, Tennessee, from brain cancer. She was fifty-four years old.

The Strides She Made

Wilma Rudolph became a symbol for underprivileged women. She was challenged, economically, physically, emotionally, and racially. Yet, she did not allow any of these to keep her from pursuing her dreams. Since then, many athletes have defied the odds and gone to overcome their physical disabilities to win medals at Olympics and other major events. Wilma Rudolph showed very clearly that if you believe in yourself, anything is possible.

Aung San Suu Kyi

Civil Rights Leader

- Born in 1945 in Myanmar (also known as Burma)
- Democratic Leader under house arrest from 1989 to 2010
- Offers the global community an awe inspiring model of how to peacefully engage complexity and tyranny
- Awarded the Nobel Peace prize in 1991

Aung San Suu Kyi keeps the flame of democracy alive in Myanmar. Suu Kyi's struggle is one of the most extraordinary examples of civil courage in Asia in recent decades. She has become an important symbol in the struggle against oppression and was awarded the Nobel Peace Prize in 1991.

Hers is a story of a woman overcoming incredible obstacles: economic hardship, religious persecution, political oppression, and even the threat of violence and death, in order to peacefully achieve great respect for human rights in her country and around the world.

Birth and Family Life in Burma

When Aung San Suu Kyi was born in Rangoon, Myanmar, in 1945, her father, General Aung San led the movement toward Burmese independence after three years of Japanese rule and more than a century of intervention and domination by the British. General Aung San returned from the war a beloved and respected national hero. He founded the modern Burmese army. He was assassinated by his rivals in 1947; Suu was only two years old when her father was assassinated.

The name "Aung San Suu Kyi" means "a bright collection of strange victories." She grew up with her mother, Ma Khin Kyi, and two brothers in Rangoon. From her father's example, Suu learned to be deeply devoted to the good of her country. Ma Khin Kyi never spoke with hatred of her husband's assassins nor she did she speak of revenge. From her mother, Aung San Suu learned courage and forgiveness.

In order to ensure her children would know their father's heritage, Ma Khin Kyi had close friendships and ties with the general's military and political comrades. Aung San Suu Kyi grew up in their company, listening to tales about her father and his history as a leader. She had the same sense of patriotism that her father had for his country. Rather than removing the daughter from her father's world, Ma Khin Kyi encouraged her to embrace it.

When Suu was growing up, she was very close to her brother Aung San Lin. Tragedy struck the family when Suu was seven years old. Aung San Lin drowned while playing along the banks of a lake on the family's property. The death affected Suu deeply. Perhaps her brother's death reinforced her philosophy of living in the moment. Nothing was forever. It would also be an early test of parting with loved ones... for years later, she would spend much of her adult life away from her husband and two children.

Aung San Suu's family taught her to be open-minded about religious beliefs. Although the family was Buddhist, Suu's maternal grandfather was a Christian. Aung San Suu read the Bible and stories from the Jathaka, or talks about the Buddhist life, which planted early seeds of Buddhism in her. Buddhism spoke of love towards people and animals and non-violence. Later on, her democratic movement for peace would be entirely based on the Buddhist principles of nonviolence and kindness to all people, even enemies.

A Mother's Influence

Ma Khin Kyi was a perfectionist and highly disciplined. From early on, the traits of focus and discipline were embedded in Aung San Suu Kyi, too. She had a way of disciplining herself to accomplishing the things that she considered important in her life. Having specific goals and aims was embedded in her from an early age.

Ma Khin Kyi believed in serving others and gaining satisfaction from giving rather than taking. She believed in the importance of not being a coward and she taught her children to face their fears head on and conquer them. The traits of courage and fearlessness would play an important role in Aung San Suu Kyi's later life. She would stand, with her head high when guns were being pointed at her by the army; she would expose the oppression imposed upon the Burmese people; and she would talk the truth fearlessly.

Moving to India

From an early age, Aung San Suu Kyi had goals. Suu went through different beliefs deciding what she wanted to be when she grew up. The influence of seeing and talking to her father's old military comrades made her decide at the age of ten that she would go into the army. She thought that would be a most honorable way to serve her country. Although she never held a gun or physically joined the army, she would later on become a warrior and fight non-violently. A few years later, Suu's love of books made her abandon the army idea and decide she would become a writer.

In 1960, Suu's mother was appointed ambassador to India. She was the first woman in Burmese history to serve as the head of a diplomatic mission and so fifteen-year-old Suu and her family moved to New Delhi. This removed Aung San Suu from her friends in Myanmar. She had to get used to a new country, a new home, and a new way of life, which made her more flexible and adaptable. Suu embraced the changes rather than rejecting them and this trait of malleability would play an important role as many surprising changes would await her in her adult years, when she deviated from the traditional road that was expected of a Burmese woman.

Aung San Suu Kyi experienced an ever-changing and flowing life. The physical and emotional vicissitudes of her early life prepared her for the rugged journey that lay ahead. It also prepared her to face challenges and to choose the difficult path rather than finding the easy path. She embraced her ever changing lifestyle.

Her stay in India would become an important part of her approach to life to fighting for democracy in Myanmar. One of the most important things that Aung

San Suu Kyi gained from her studies during this period was her discovery of the methods and philosophy of the great Indian leader, Mahatma Gandhi. He had become famous for his use of nonviolent action to win political goals. By staying in India, Aung San Suu Kyi was actually able to "feel" his non-violent spirit. She would embrace his philosophy and use his tools for her own political crusade later on.

Marriage Outside her Culture

In 1964, Aung San Suu left India to study at Hughes College, one of the five women's colleges at Oxford University in England. There, she met Michael Aris, a British student. Marriages of people from different ethnic and cultural backgrounds were not accepted in Myanmar. Suu was the daughter of the most famous Burmese national hero and would have been expected to marry another Burmese citizen.

Aung San Suu could have rejected any courtship with the Englishman. Yet, the fact that she consented to a relationship indicated her desire to explore the road less traveled in marriage. Her decision to break away from Burmese tradition and marry someone outside of her culture, thus creating rifts within her own family, showed courage in following her heart. Suu loved Aris as a human being, not as an Englishman, and that was all that mattered. Later on, though, the Burmese Government would accuse her of betraying her own culture by marrying a non-Burmese.

As an educated, free-thinking woman who was beginning to think for herself instead of being told what to do by her parents, society, and everyone else, Suu wanted to be with a man who would allow her to continue with her ability to think rather than constrict her life with household chores and motherhood. It was also a reflection of her desire to do something that most Burmese women would not dare do. By marrying an Englishman, Suu was flushing out an old system and giving birth to a new one. She would attempt to do the same politically for Myanmar.

Flying to Myanmar

Marriage, motherhood, travel, and academic life had interrupted any thoughts Aung San Suu might have had about pursuing a career in either the political or diplomatic fields. Yet, Myanmar was always on her mind. She knew only too well how difficult and complicated politics were. Her father had been worn down trying to unite all of the groups that wanted a voice in the government. Still, there was a restlessness in her that none of the other things she did seemed to satisfy.

In March 1988, Suu received a call from Myanmar. Her mother had suffered a stroke and was in a hospital. Aung San Suu Kyi made immediate preparations to fly to Burma. In the months since she had returned to care for her mother, she was aware of the growing unrest and turmoil in the country. After her mother's death, Suu remained in Myanmar.

In the years after Myanmar achieved independence in 1948, the country went through a difficult time of social and economic problems as the Burmese took over governing themselves. There were many disagreements between the various ethnic and political groups. A general named Ne Win stepped in to try and hold the country together. In March 1962, Ne Win staged a successful military coup. That year his Myanmar Socialist Program Party seized control of Myanmar's government. This was the beginning of Ne Win's military dictatorship, which would last for the next twenty-six years. He suspended the constitution that had been drawn up by General Aung San and his committee years ago. Myanmar was not a democracy any longer.

If anyone tried to protest against the government, General Ne Win used his army to silence them with immediate arrest, then imprisonment, or sentences of death without trial. Buddhist monks and Burmese citizens began to join in the demonstrations. The protests became bold and spread from Rangoon to other areas. Burmese students had started demonstrating in protest marches against General Ne Win's government. They demanded radical political change. Rioting broke out.

"The value systems of those with access to power and of those far removed from such access cannot be the same. The viewpoint of the privileged is unlike that of the underprivileged."

General Ne Win sealed off the country from contact with the outside world. Promoting an isolationist policy that he called the "Burmese Way to Socialism," he expelled foreign journalists, suppressed any freedom of the press, nationalized most industrial and economic institutions, throttled the press, and established a police state.

Unemployment soared. As the economy continued to decline, violence erupted. Myanmar was in a constant of civil war. In 1988, Ne Win resigned as head of his party. He was replaced by another military leader.

The fiery situation came to a head on August 8, 1988. The country was put under martial law because thousands of students and other citizens had started demonstrating in the streets.

"It cannot be doubted that in most countries today women, in comparison to men, still remain underprivileged."

In Rangoon, a peaceful demonstration was held with thousands of people of all ages, economic groups, and professions. There were students, farmers, laborers, members of the armed forces, Buddhist monks, Christians, Muslims, businesspeople, artists, and homemakers. Aung San Suu Kyi later explained what united the people of Myanmar on this day, namely, a desire for change: "They wanted no more of the authoritarian rule...that had impoverished (Myanmar) intellectually, politically, morally, and economically." The army troops fired on the unarmed demonstrators — more than 3,000 people were killed. The day became known as the "massacre of 8-8-88."

On September 18, 1988, the army, under the leadership of a general named Saw Maung, staged a coup — the second in Myanmar's recent history — and took over control of the government. Anyone who was arrested could be sentenced to prison without a trial. Open opposition to the new government was crushed through the use of brutal force. In taking power, the State Law and Order Restoration Council (SLORC) stated that military control would be temporary. They said that free elections would be held once law and order was reestablished. They allowed the formation of new political parties. Aung San Suu Kyi was in Myanmar at the time and, with the massacre of 8-8-88 in her mind, she knew she could not remain silent about what was happening.

Getting into Politics

Aung San Suu Kyi's return to her country had not gone unnoticed by political activists, many of whom turned to her for advice because she was the well-known daughter of the most famous freedom fighter in Burmese history. She offered words of inspiration. "Peace as a goal is an ideal which will not be contested by any government or nation, not even the most belligerent," said Suu.

On the late morning of August 26, 1988, Aung San Suu gathered in the grounds of the gold encrusted Shwedagon Pagoda, one of the most sacred and revered Buddhist temples in Myanmar, that presides over Rangoon and addressed a crowd estimated at between 300,000 and one million people. As a result of this speech, she emerged as the active figurehead of an oppressed people. Entering politics was not an ambition she had set out to accomplish and life would never be the same again for this vibrant and bold woman.

Aung San Suu announced her decision to enter the struggle for democracy. Her resemblance to her father and the words she used to describe "(Myanmar's) second struggle for independence" inspired the people to follow her leadership. "I could not, as my father's daughter, remain indifferent to all that was going on. This national crisis could in fact be called the second struggle for national independence," Suu said.

Aung San Suu urged not only for both the military and demonstrators to refrain from any more violence, but also that the government release all the people they had imprisoned over the last few months. The movement began to gather enormous support. In her inspired campaign, Suu advanced in the footsteps of Mahatma Gandhi and Martin Luther King, employing tactics of non-violence and civil disobedience in pursuit of democracy. Her essential message of self-responsibility, rooted in Buddhism, developed into a high-minded political ideology that she calls Myanmar's "Revolution of the Spirit."

"The struggle for democracy and human rights in (Myanmar) is a struggle for life and dignity. It is a struggle that encompasses our political, social, and economic aspirations."

The people listened carefully. They needed someone to lead them. Aung San Suu talked about a free Myanmar and about democracy. "It is my aim to help the people in (Myanmar) to attain democracy without further violence or loss of life," she said. What was offensive to her was the military regime's denial of "the full enjoyment of human rights," which undermined any notion of full independence. That the people had demonstrated their desire for democracy was overwhelmingly apparent from the uprising that began in 8.8.88. Said Suu:

"Let us not be disunited. Let us resolve to march forward in unity toward our cherished goal. In doing so please use peaceful means. If a people or a nation can reach their objectives by discipline and peaceful means, it would be a most honorable and admirable achievement."

"Human beings the world over need freedom and security that they may be able to realize their full potential."

Aung San Suu traveled throughout Myanmar to organize the citizens for democracy. In many towns her life was at risk. She was not afraid to criticize the government. She spoke out boldly against the military killings, the imprisonments, and the violations of human rights. She did this, even at the onset of death.

On one occasion Aung San Suu and some of her supporters had been walking down the middle of the road, returning from a small town where she had given a political speech to rally citizens. Suddenly a military jeep pulled in front of them. An army captain shouted at her and her supporters to get off the road. The captain said the troops would shoot if they walked. She marched right up to the soldiers.

She stood defiantly as everyone waited to see what would happen. Her body was rigid and unbending. She knew that if she gave in to this intimidation, then she would go on being intimidated. She later said, "I thought, 'What does one do? Does one turn back or keep going?' My thought was 'one doesn't turn back in situations like this.'" She stood still. The soldiers cocked their guns. The seconds ticked by and tensions mounted, but she remained calm as she stared at the soldiers. Suddenly, the army in command rushed up and gave an order for the soldiers to lower their guns. Aung San Suu Kyi and her group walked through the still-kneeling soldiers. Once again, she had demonstrated her commitment and courage to fight for the truth.

"Nonviolence means positive action. You have to work for whatever you want. You don't just sit there doing nothing and hope to get what you want," said Suu.

From this suffocating darkness came a glimmer of hope, as a new leader emerged. Her political party became the first ray of hope for the oppressed Burmese people. Emerging as a natural leader, Aung San Suu Kyi co-founded the National League for Democracy (NLD) to run against the military party. She became a rallying point for the people as she encouraged them to fight for their rights and a free democratic government.

Aung San Suu was campaigning with other members of her political party, the National League for Democracy when this confrontation occurred. They were preparing for an upcoming election in Myanmar. Aung San Suu Kyi did not believe that the government had any intention of allowing free elections to be held, but she still joined with other leaders of the freedom movement to create a political party called The National League for Democracy (NLD).

"The people adore her. Everywhere she goes, they bedeck her with flowers — roses, jasmine, chrysanthemums," Terry McCarthy, reporting in *The Independent*, May 1989.

"Fear is not the natural state of civilized people."

The government continued its harassment of both Aung San Suu Kyi and her supporters. They attacked her personally, telling many lies about her in order to turn people against her. They said she worked for their countries and was betraying the Burmese people.

On June 20, 1989, the Burmese Government announced that under martial law they had the right to detain anyone for up to three years without any charges being filed or a trial being held.

On May 27, 1990, elections were held and Aung San Suu Kyi's NLD party won a landslide victory, taking 392 of the 485 seats contested, more than eighty percent of the constituencies. However, she had already been detained under house arrest before the elections, which took place on July 20, 1989. Instead of transferring power to the elected representatives as promised, the military commanders instigated a nationwide crackdown. The military responded by reasserting its control over the government. It banned all political gatherings.

House Arrest

Throughout the period Aung San Suu Kyi was under house arrest, the government let her know that she could have her freedom, but she would have to leave the country and would never be allowed to return. She refused her own freedom because she would never abandon the citizens of Myanmar.

Suu was imprisoned in her own home for six years. During that time, she was not allowed to see anyone. For more than two years, she didn't even see her husband and two sons. Life would never again be the same for this family. The government canceled her children's visas to enter the country; only her husband was allowed to come back. Aris died on his fifty-third birthday, March 27, 1999, but Suu remained separated from her children, who lived in the United Kingdom.

"Sometimes I didn't even have enough money to eat. I became so weak from malnourishment that my hair fell out, and I couldn't get out of bed," Suu said.

The sacrifices Suu had made for her commitment to non-violence and belief in freedom gained her worldwide admiration and respect. Through her story, people around the world began to understand and feel the suffering of the people in Myanmar. From July 20, 1989, to November 10, 2010, Aung San Suu Kyi was under house arrest for her democratic efforts in Myanmar.

Nobel Prize

Aung San Suu was awarded the Nobel Peace Prize in 1991. She became the seventieth individual to win the Nobel Peace Prize and only the eighth woman to be selected for this award. The decision of the Nobel Committee mentions: "The Norwegian Nobel Committee has decided to award the Nobel Peace Prize for 1991 to Aung San Suu Kyi of Myanmar (Burma) for her non-violent struggle for democracy and human rights."

When her son Alexander accepted the Nobel Peace Prize on behalf of his mother, he was only eighteen years old. He included a quote from his mother in the acceptance speech: "To live the full life…one must have the courage to bear the responsibility of the needs of others."

In 1992, Suu became the recipient of the Simon Bolivar Prize, given by UNESCO in 1995. The Jawaharlal Nehru and Gandhi awards were given to her in 1996. Suu has always indicated that her acceptance of these honors was on behalf of the Burmese people, not herself.

Myanmar Today

Several thousand prisoners remain incarcerated in Burmese prisons today. Relentless ethnic cleansing and the murder, torture, and rape of minorities have left more than 3,000 villages destroyed. Nearly one million refugees have fled the country and one million more internally displaced, subsisting in primitive, malaria infested jungle conditions. Hundreds of thousands of Burmese citizens are enslaved as forced laborers building roads, bridges, dams, and monuments for tourism. Millions more are tyrannized by one of the largest standing armies in the world. Some of the army members are children as young as eleven years.

There have been spiritually-led revolutions where soldiers have fired at peaceful protesters. The military dictatorship is still in power. International outcry has resulted in little change.

It is Aung San Suu Kyi's goal to bring democracy to Myanmar and restore Myanmar's reputation as a country of beauty rather than turmoil; a country of educated citizens rather than uneducated, impoverished individuals; a wealthy country of financial resources rather than a poor country of corruption and greed. She hopes that by her example, the people will also become dedicated to the fight for a democratic government.

On April 1, 2012, her opposition party, the National League for Democracy, announced that Aung San Suu Kyi was elected to the Pyithu Hluttaw, the lower house of the Burmese parliament, representing the constituency of Kawhmu. Her party also won forty-three of the forty-five vacant seats in the lower house.

Suu's Vision

Myanmar's struggle for democratic freedom is in fact a microcosm of the larger picture of a free-thinking society: The world's struggle to overcome tyranny, to end violence, and to establish free societies. Ultimately, the revolution in Burma is a challenge to us all; namely, the voice of democratic decency everywhere versus the machinery of repression.

Throughout her years of persecution, Aung San Suu has continually stressed the importance of everyday revolution and the art and activism of expressing liberation through living. She believes that love is an action, not a state of mind. It is not enough to just sit there and send thoughts of loving kindness. One must put that love into action. She says it takes courage to lift one's eyes up from their own needs and to see the truth of the world around them, a truth, such as Myanmar, where there are no human rights. It takes even more courage not to turn away, to make excuses for noninvolvement, or to be corrupted by fear. It takes courage to feel the truth, to feel one's conscience.

Aung San Suu Kyi's nonviolent revolution of the spirit offers the global community an awe-inspiring model of how to peacefully engage complexity and tyranny. It offers the potential to bring about true social and political change. Aung San Suu is a dynamic woman with an unshakable conviction, inseparable from her principles and sustained by a sense of justice and duty. The one quality that best defines her is sincerity. She is a seeker, one who makes her life a vehicle for an awakening to deeper and greater truths. She is straight and direct. She is a woman who enjoys her sovereignty and happiness while fighting for the independence of others. Aung San Suu Kyi has become a public figure, and a woman to be reckoned with, in a specific time in a specific place.

The Strides She Made

"Feel always free," Aung San Suu Kyi encourages everyone who dares to enter the revolution. "Nobody can detain your mind, though they can detain your body. Master your mind and nobody can abuse you."

Aung San Suu is a symbol of the greatness Myanmar can become if freedom of speech were to persist. She is the hope that Myanmar needs to become a great nation. People are afraid. Aung San Suu Kyi has stepped up to hold their hands literally and figuratively. She has created change by acting on her nonviolent beliefs. She gives hope to women who are raped, children who are molested, and mothers who are forever grief stricken by the disappearances of their sons. Aung San Suu Kyi lies at the heart of Myanmar's revolution. She is a life-transforming metaphor, a candle of hope illuminating a totalitarian darkness. It reveals an invitation to rise in spirit and take action; an invitation to support not just Myanmar and Aung San Suu Kyi, but the message of freedom and the belief in hope.

Aung San Suu offers insight into the courage of the Burmese people. Despite her silence and isolation, both her voice and her presence infuse them with strength and a vision of freedom. "Those of us who decided to work for democracy in (Myanmar)," she explains, "made our choice in the conviction that the danger of standing up for basic human rights in a repressive society was preferable to the safety of a quiescent life in servitude. Ours is a nonviolent movement that depends on faith in the human predilection for fair play and compassion."

If not for women like Aung San Suu Kyi, Myanmar might as well be completely erased from the global map, as isolationist policy leaders would treat the country like a burial ground for a handful of short-sighted leaders with limited vision. Aung San Suu Kyi is a woman of vision, a bright, smart woman who will pick up the lives of battered women and men throughout Myanmar and start the healing process that is so vital for this country to begin its journey towards greatness.

Meryl Streep

A Leading Lady in Hollywood

- Born June 22, 1949, in New Jersey
- As a child she felt insecure about her "odd" looks
- Leading American actress who has worked in theater, television, and film
- Nominated for seventeen Academy Awards, winner of three
- Nominated for twenty-six Golden Globe awards, winner of eight
- A devoted mother and wife

With her extraordinary versatility, impressive technique, and astonishing emotional range, Meryl Streep swept Hollywood off its feet in the late 1970s, becoming one of the most accomplished actors of our time. With seventeen Academy Award nominations (she's won three) and twenty-six Golden Globe nominations (she's won eight), Streep has received more nominations than any other actor in the history of either award. Her work has also earned her two Emmy Awards, two Screen Actors Guild Awards, a Cannes Film Festival award, and five New York Film Critics Circle Awards.

Yet, by her own admission, Streep's teenage years were seeped in self-consciousness and "what boys thought of her." Enrolling in an all-girl's college made the difference in her life. It was a blessing that changed her perspectives and expectations of life...

Birth and Background

On June 22, 1949, in Summit, New Jersey, Mary Louise Streep gave birth to her first child, a round baby girl whose biggest booster was her father. Meryl's father wanted to name the baby after his wife, "the woman who made it all possible."

Mary Louise Streep (later Meryl Streep) impressed no one with her star quality as a child. She wore heavy spectacles and a dental brace. She had pudgy cheeks and the crooked nose that now lends a special quality to her profile looked distinctly odd on her young face. A pair of grown-up glasses formed a permanent ridge on her nose. Meryl, her nickname from birth, had few close friends as a child; she was convinced that her parents were the only people in the world who loved her.

Meryl's hair was mousy brown and frizzy. It was trimmed at home around the kitchen table, which always left Meryl with a short, funny fringe on her forehead. Her odd looks marred her childhood. She felt that she was always too big for her age. She recalls an ugly incident when some neighborhood kids chased her up a tree and hit her legs until they bled.

"'I was bossy, prim, and determined. I looked like a middle-aged woman. The other kids thought I was one of the teachers,'" said Meryl of her growing up years.

Meryl Streep came from a well-to-do family. Her father, Harry Streep II, was an advertising executive with a pharmaceutical company. Her mother, Mary Louise, was a commercial artist working from home. For the most part, it was a comfortable and uneventful childhood. Meryl's parents cushioned her from the harsh realities of the world and were over-protective.

The Streeps were devoted, all-American parents striving for life, liberty, happiness, and a big backyard. Harry II stayed late at work and hoped for bonuses. Mary Louise freelanced as an illustrator. Soon after the birth of Meryl's two brothers, they were able to move to wealthier communities in New Jersey. Each time they sold their house, they made a profit. Their financial planning was an economic lesson on how to move from middle class to upper middle class in a few easy, well-planned steps. It was the American Dream coming true, slowly but steadily. Streep recalls a girl who lived up the street from them who had a Native American sampler, a cross-stitch, on her wall:

"It said: 'Do not judge another man until you have walked a mile in his moccasins.' That was something that really struck with me; to walk in somebody else's shoes, to feel like somebody else."

High School Insecurities

At the beginning, Meryl didn't fit in. Until high school she found herself "barely presentable," at least, that is what she felt about herself. From an early age she started doing impressions of people. Her high school years were filled with insecurities. Boys were the context in which the whole female world arranged itself.

In high school, Meryl did musicals. She had a good singing voice and thought she would study music in college. She got her first applause by age twelve when she sang "O Holy Night" in French at her school's Christmas concert. Her mother thought that Meryl's talent was "too good to waste" and started taking her for voice lessons with a professional teacher.

Naturally, Meryl's high school friends and associates assumed she would become a musical actress, but Meryl didn't think so. "I just didn't think I had the kind of energy to do that," she said, and so she began to consider drama as a hobby. However, she was the first to admit that "I never saw a real play, a serious one, until I was in one."

Meryl's last year of high school postponed any serious considerations about her future. She had other things on her mind, boys being one of them. In her senior year, she was crowned homecoming queen at the prom. There was nothing else she could achieve, or so she thought, as a teenager who had just completed high school.

"There is More to Life than Dating"

Meryl felt like herself only when she went to college. She went to Vassar College, an all-girl's college, where she was able to find her own individuality and be herself. She arrived "interested in boys when everybody here was female. I think that was the single, most important catalyst for change in my life to that point," she commented in her later years. This was the cause of her internal transformation: to not have to worry about boys and what boys thought of her. She met wonderful women at Vassar.

Meryl's days at Vassar were spent exploring hopes and dreams, not just coloring nails and reading teen magazines on how to attract boys. Being in an all-girl's college contributed to making her feel comfortable in her own skin as a woman: high school was all about conforming to existing ideals while college was all about making up her own ideal about who she wanted to be.

Meryl began to regret her "petty concerns" in high school. In high school, there was generally one acceptable way to be and it was dictated by the superficial rules of dating. "There are those people who try to be that way, and there are the other, clunky, disastrously uncool individuals, the nerds, who swim upstream in those waters," she remarked about her high school years.

Vassar changed Meryl's life for the better. It was at Vassar that her change in thinking and her growth of mind and imagination took place. Surrounded by brainy women who spent their evenings in the library, Meryl engaged in intellectual discussions. "I felt absolutely great in that atmosphere and I blossomed," she has said. "At Vassar, it was commonplace to give your best shot, so that became a habit. I learned to believe in myself. I acquired a genuine sense of identity."

When Meryl got to Vassar, she saw very quickly how many students in the music department were also good at math and that quickly dissuaded her from becoming a music major. Instead, she followed a liberal arts study. Meryl also enrolled as an exchange student at Dartmouth College for a quarter before it became coeducational. She also appeared off-Broadway while still attending Vassar College.

Meryl received her Bachelor of Arts at Vassar College in 1971 in drama and costume design.

Yale and After College Years

Money was tighter than ever before in the Streep household. Both her brothers were in college. Meryl survived financially with the help of a scholarship to Yale, which recognized her talent and worked her to the bone. While at Yale, she played a variety of roles on the stage, including the glamorous Helena in *A Midsummer Night's Dream*. Meryl played in forty productions during her three years at Yale. She also fought with her teachers, developed an ulcer, and visited a psychiatrist.

Meryl Streep subsequently earned an MFA from Yale School of Drama. She had a degree in her right pocket, another one in her left, an ulcer in her stomach, and no job. The real world after college was coming upon her.

Meryl auditioned for the Theater Communications Group (TCG) and the calls for different roles began to come in. She joined the Green Mountain Summer Repertory Group in Woodstock, Vermont, where she both acted and directed. Meryl made her professional stage debut in "The Playboy of Seville" (1971) and her screen debut in the television movie *Deadliest Season* (1977). In that same year, she made her film debut with *Julia* (1977).

Personal Losses and Gains

Meryl was living in New York City with a friend named John Cazale, who had been diagnosed with bone cancer. He was cast in *The Deer Hunter*

(1978) and Streep was delighted to secure a small role because it allowed her to remain with Cazale for the duration of filming. She was not specifically interested in the part, commenting, "They needed a girl between the two guys and I was it."

The death of John Cazale in 1978 brought great grief to her. Her carefully constructed world fell apart. The golden girl had to mature beyond her twenty-six years to find the inner resources to cope with her tragic loss. Soon after John died, she also lost her home. Six months later, Meryl married Donald Gummer, a sculptor.

Becoming a Star

Both critical and commercial success came quickly with roles in *The Deer Hunter* (1978) and *Kramer vs. Kramer* (1979), the former giving Meryl her first Academy Award nomination and the latter, her first win. "Acting is being susceptible to what is around you and it's letting it all come in. Acting is a clearing away of everything except what you want and need, and it's wonderful in that way. And when it's right, you are lost in the moment," she said.

In New York City, Meryl appeared in Tennessee Williams' "27 Wagons Full of Cotton" and Arthur Miller's "A Memory of Two Mondays." For the former, she received a Tony Award nomination for Best Featured Actress in a Play. Her other early Broadway credits include Anton Chekhov's "The Cherry Orchard" and the Bertolt Brecht-Kurt Weill musical "Happy End," in which she originally appeared off-Broadway at the Chelsea Theater Center.

As the Polish Holocaust survivor in *Sophie's Choice* (1982), Meryl's emotional dramatic performance and her apparent mastery of a Polish accent drew praise. She won the Best Actress Oscar for *Sophie's Choice*. Her ability to master any accent and to inhibit characters of any background and era is remarkable.

Throughout the 1980s, Meryl's virtuoso performances dominated the box office. She starred in *The French Lieutenant's Woman* (1981) and created memorable characters in such diverse films as *Silkwood*, *Falling in Love*, *Out of Africa*, and *A Cry in the Dark*. She received an Academy Award for Best Actress nomination in 1996 for her performance in the film, *The Bridges of Madison County*. It tells the story of a married but lonely Italian woman living in the 1960s in Madison County, Iowa. The lonely war-bride, played by Meryl, engages in a four-day love affair with a *National Geographic* photographer who is visiting Madison County in order to create a photographic essay on the covered bridges in the area.

"The great gift of human beings is that we have the power of empathy."

Streep won the Academy Award for Best Actress for her performance in *The Iron Lady* (2011), a British biographical film based on the life of Margaret Thatcher, the longest serving Prime Minister of the United Kingdom of the twentieth century. It digs into the discomfort that both men and women feel when a woman reaches a role of power and leadership. The film begins with the elderly Lady Thatcher buying milk unrecognized by other customers and walking back from the shop alone. She struggles with dementia and the lack of power that comes with the aging process. She looks back on defining moments of her personal and professional life. She is shown as having difficulty distinguishing between the past and present, a theme throughout the film is the personal price that Thatcher has paid for power.

While the film met with mixed reviews, Meryl's performance was widely acclaimed and considered to be one of the finest of her career. She received her seventeenth Academy Award nomination and, ultimately, the Academy Award for Best Actress for her portrayal of Thatcher across four decades.

Managing Marriage and an Impressive Career

Meryl puts her family first. A devoted mother, she has sidestepped the fast-paced Hollywood life and is mindful of her family as she chooses her roles. She has passed on roles that would have taken her too far away from her family for too long. Unless the film project has a quality that excites her, Meryl Streep would rather stay at home. "It's always better to be authentically yourself. All these things are a part of learning how to live with other people," she has said.

Meryl has aired her views on the subject of privacy and the media, sometimes to the brink of paranoia. She has been known to walk out on insensitive interviewers and is careful about talking about her family life in public. "It seems to me," she told one journalist, "that when you become famous a lot of your energy goes into maintaining what you had before you were famous, maintaining your sense of observation, being able to look at other people. If they take away your powers of observation, you are lost."

Meryl has also said that "grabbing the cold gold at the Oscars was great, but it didn't come close to being handed my first-born — or my fourth-born for that matter."

Meryl seems genuinely mystified and irritated by the trappings of international stardom, as it does not sit easily on her shoulders. She is a reluctant superstar ever to capture the imagination of the American public and this hesitancy may be her biggest appeal. Her shy manner refuses to break hearts. She won't relinquish her down-to-earth ways. In all her roles, Meryl forces emotion out of simple truth. She refuses to upstage reality and avoids "the big display."

The Strides She Made

In film after film, Meryl Streep manages to present a different facet of herself. She is the kind of actress who prefers to bury herself deep inside a character, to obscure and mask her own identity. Meryl is Meryl, totally unique, her own woman, dependent not on any spurious recollection of screen idols past or present, but on a bedrock of confidence, talent, technique, and dedication. It is this quest for excellence that has characterized her work to date. As her career gathered momentum, the roles became bigger and more challenging.

Meryl Streep has crafted a career playing an incredible assortment of complex women. Off-screen, she has demonstrated quite a range as well — as wife, mother, activist, and advocate for improving the status of women in Hollywood.

Meryl Streep herself is an "Iron Lady." Her "iron"-like qualities are balanced by her gentleness and kind genuineness. Meryl is gentle but tough. She is a lady who is true to her beliefs, firm in defending her privacy, and a loving mother. She is widely regarded as one of the most talented actresses of all time.

Mother Teresa

Shining God's Radiance for the Poor Masses

· Born in 1910

· In 1950, founded the Missionaries of Charity in Calcutta, India

· Became a nun among the destitute masses of the Calcutta slums

· Beatified by Pope John Paul II and given the title Blessed Teresa of Calcutta

· Won the Nobel Peace Prize in 1979 and India's highest civilian honor, the Bharat Ratna, in 1980 for her humanitarian work

· Died in 1997

Mother Teresa saw beauty in the ugly. What many would consider repugnant and abhor, she lovingly wrapped her arms around. Hatred could not fester in her heart.

> *"The more repugnant the work, the greater the effect of love and cheerful service. If I had not first picked up the woman whose face and legs were eaten by rats, I could not have been a Missionary of Charity. Feelings of repugnance are human."*

Mother Teresa gave the world unbridled hope. She was there for the poor and rich alike. She founded the Missionaries of Charity, which was, in her own words, to care for "the hungry, the naked, the homeless, the crippled, the blind, the lepers, all those people who feel unwanted, unloved, uncared for throughout society, and people that have become a burden to the society and are shunned by everyone."

God sent Mother Teresa to be his light. He invited her to pitch her tent in the blackest of places, so that she might shine with his radiance. She became a reflection of God's glory in miniature. Mother Teresa's inner and outer world was a place in which the brilliance of God's light and the bleakness of man's darkness met. In this meeting point, her victorious light shone. It all began with a simple calling that she received, on a train ride to Darjeeling, India.

Birth and Background

Mother Teresa began life as Gonxha Agnes Bojaxhiu, the youngest of three children of an Albanian family born August 26, 1910, in Macedonia. Her father died in 1919 when she was only eight years old. She was inspired by reports sent home from West Bengal, India, by Jesuit missionaries. The Sisters of Loreta were doing missionary work there. She left home at the age of eighteen to join the Sisters of Loreto as a missionary. She would never see her mother or sister again.

In 1929, she arrived in Calcutta, alone, with just five Rupees (about $0.05 cents) on her. That was more than enough for her, because the foundation for her greatness as a human being was spiritual, not material. She taught us that money should not be a prerequisite for doing greatness in this world of helping others. A large heart of kindness is far greater than a large bank account. She was assigned to the Loreta Convent and began teaching geography in their middle school. Not knowing the language posed no obstacle for Mother Teresa. She was always ready for a challenge, to explore something different. She mastered the Bengali language.

God Calls Mother Teresa

On September 10, 1946, following her yearly custom, Mother Theresa left Calcutta for eight days of spiritual retreat. During that train ride to Darjeeling, India, somewhere along the way, Mother Theresa had an extraordinary experience of God. In her characteristic humility, she would refer to this life-changing experience as "a call within a call" to leave Loreto and to go into the slums of Calcutta. She ventured into the slums on the other side of the convent hall.

Not having any medical training did not dissuade her from embarking on her humanitarian cause. She spent a few months in Patna to receive a basic medical training in the Holy Family Hospital.

Mother Teresa began her missionary work in 1948, replacing her traditional Loreto habit with a humble cotton sari, which would become her emblem. Her sari was simple, white, and decorated with a blue border. Her selection of colors was not accidental; it would become the basis of what she did. White symbolized purity, love, transparency, and sanctity. There was nothing to hide in what she did. Everything was as naked and raw as it could get. There were no facades or pretensions.

Typically, women wear the color blue when they are seeking calm and relaxation to counteract chaos or agitation, to open the flow of communication, to learn new things, and to seek solitude and peace. Blue also symbolizes the Virgin Mary and is the color of inspiration, sincerity, and spirituality. In essence, the habit that Mother Teresa wore symbolized everything that she represented in her calling.

As word spread of her one-woman outreach to the poor, people who had known her in Loreto began contributing to her new mission. There, on the outskirts of the city, began the slums that became Mother Teresa's Calcutta. This would be Mother Teresa's domain for the rest of her days; her meeting place with God in the poor and our meeting place with God in her.

What the Sisters in Sari Did

By the 1950s, the Sisters in their Blue-bordered White saris were a distinctive part of the great sprawling city. They trooped out in the morning, two by two, to feed homeless families, chiefly refugees, to a dozen slum schools, to the Home for the Dying, and to children's clinics in the worst slums. These included hospices and homes for people with HIV/AIDS, tuberculosis, soup kitchens, children's and family counseling programs, personal helpers, orphanages, and schools.

In the Home for the Dying, Mother Teresa and her Sisters leaned over cadaverous men and women, feeding them slowly and gently. Mother Teresa went from patient to patient, sitting beside them, and giving them human comfort by holding their hands or stroking their heads.

The Sisters in Sari or the Missionaries of Charity also established several leprosy outreach clinics throughout Calcutta, providing medication, bandages and food. "We cannot let a child of God die like an animal in the gutter," Mother Teresa declared. When asked how she could face this agony and serve these suffering people day after day, she answered, "To me, each one is Christ; Christ in a distressing disguise."

The Calcutta Landscape

To gain a better idea of what Mother Teresa faced, take a closer look at one of the more famous of Calcutta's slums, the ironically named "City of Joy." Calcutta once claimed one of the densest concentrations of humanity on the planet with 200,000 people per square mile:

"It was a place where there was not even one tree for three thousand inhabitants, without a single flower, a butterfly, a bird, apart from vultures and crows, it was a place where children did not even know what a bush, a forest, or a pond was, where the air was so laden with carbon dioxide and sulfur that pollution killed at least one member in every family; a place where men and beasts baked in a furnace for the eight months of summer until the monsoon transformed their alleyways and shacks into lakes of mud and excrement; a place where leprosy,

tuberculosis, dysentery and all the malnutrition diseases, until recently, reduced the average life expectancy to one of the lowest in the world; a place where eighty-five hundred cows and buffalo tied up to dung heaps provided milk infected with germs. Above all, however, it was a place where the most extreme economic poverty ran rife. Nine out of ten of its inhabitants did not have a single rupee per day with which to buy half a pound of rice…. Considered a dangerous neighborhood with a terrible reputation, the haunt of Untouchables, pariahs, social rejects, it was a world apart, living apart from the world." (Dominique LaPierre, The City of Joy, p. 46)

With over sixteen million inhabitants, Calcutta is notorious for its pavement dwellers, street children, scavengers, and diseases. Many start their day on the sidewalks, huddled under cardboard and tattered cloth. Down on the sidewalk, men squat on the cracked cement, smoking bidis and shooing flies. Along the sides of the road, rickshaw pullers run, swallowed up in smoke and traffic. Barefoot men push their handcarts, piled high, bound for market. They trudge on, amid clouds of mosquitoes, incessant horns, and the non-stop buffeting of passing trucks and speeding buses.

The following is a true story that Mother Teresa encountered:

"One day I picked up a man from the gutter. His body was covered with worms. I brought him to our house, and what did this man say? He did not curse. He did not blame anyone. He just said, 'I've lived like an animal in the street, but I'm going to die like an angel, loved and cared for!' It took us three hours to clean him. Finally, the man looked up at the sister and said, 'Sister, I'm going home to God.' And then he died. I've never seen such a radiant smile on a human face as the one on that man's face. He went home to God. See what love can do."

It was easy for a child to get lost in Calcutta. Yet, amidst all the chaos, some children also found their way, finding even the humblest abode that they can call home. Mother Teresa remembers a little girl who seemed lost in this over-populated city, but really wasn't:

"One day I found a little girl in the street, so I took her to our children's home. We have a nice place and good food there. We gave her clean clothes and we made her as happy as we could.
After a few hours the little girl ran away. I looked for her, but I couldn't find her anywhere. Then after a few days I found her again. And, again, I brought her to our home and told a sister, 'Sister, please, follow this child wherever she goes.'

The little girl ran away again, but the sister followed to find out where she was going and why she kept running away. She followed the little girl and discovered that the little one's mother was living under a tree in the street. The mother had placed two stones there and did her cooking under that tree.

The sister sent word to me and I went there. I found joy on that little girl's face, because she was with her mother, who loved her and was making special food for her in that little open place.

I asked the little girl, 'How is it that you would not stay with us? You had so many beautiful things in our home.'

She answered: 'I could not live without my mother. She loves me.'

That little girl was happier to have the meager food her mother was cooking in the street than all the things I had given her. Her mother was her family.

Love begins at home."

Even amid such extreme poverty, Mother Teresa discovered in the poor of Calcutta a nobility of character, a vitality of family ties and cultural wealth, and an ingenuity that made her genuinely proud. "The poor are great people," she vigorously insisted. These were people she deeply admired. She insisted that the two-way exchange that passed between her and the poor of Calcutta worked in her favor; that she received much more than she gave, and was evermore blessed than she was blessing.

"My secret is very simple: I pray. Through prayer I become one in love with Christ. I realize that praying to Him is loving Him."

Serving the Poor

It was precisely to the poorest that she was sent; to the outcasts, the lepers, the hungry and naked, the "throwaways of society," as Mother Teresa called them. These were the ones for whom God most urgently longed. They were the ones who needed his love most. Mother Teresa created appreciation for the poor. "I have never seen the poor grumble or curse, nor have I seen any of them dejected with sadness. The poor are great people; they can accept very difficult things."

Wherever there is humanity, there is pain, be it in slums or prisons or palaces, and that wherever there is pain, there is Jesus. As the years went on, Mother Teresa felt moved to begin bringing the light of God's love beyond the realm of physical pain and material poverty.

Slum of the Spirit

In 1960, Mother Teresa visited Las Vegas. Like Calcutta, Las Vegas was not just another city, it was an icon; unlike Calcutta, Las Vegas, with its casinos and night life, was an icon of opulence, a poverty in a different sense. To emphasize the universal scope of her message, God was sending Mother Teresa to the other extreme, to the opposite end of the economic spectrum. He was sending her to "be his light" in an anti-Calcutta; not a slum in any classic sense, but in many ways a slum of the spirit.

"Around the world, not only in the poor countries, but I found the poverty of the West so much more difficult to remove. When I pick up a person from the street, hungry, I give him a plate of rice, a piece of bread, I have satisfied. I have removed that hunger. But a person that is shut out, that feels unwanted, unloved, terrified, the person that has been thrown out from society, that poverty is so hurtable and so much, and I find that very difficult."

Mother Teresa did not attempt to convert us to her beliefs or force a specific religion on anyone. She simply described her strong faith and told us about her work with the poor and the sick. Being a human was not about following a specific religion. Rather, it was about being a loving person. She did not pick Christians, overlooking Buddhists or Moslems. She picked up all human beings who had lost hope. Her stories are obviously not meant to convince us of her religious convictions; rather, they simply demonstrate how human beings, when given the most basic kinds of love and attention, find significant transformation and discover their humanity, dignity, and at least momentary happiness.

Those brought to the dying home received medical attention and were afforded the opportunity to die with dignity, according to the rituals of their faith. Moslems were read the Quran, Hindus received water from the Ganges, and Catholics received the Last Rites. "A beautiful death is for people who lived like animals to die like angels — loved and wanted," Mother Teresa said. "God…thirsts for us to thirst for him."

As difficult and painful as her dark night became, Mother Teresa never allowed herself to become "lost" in her darkness. She never rebelled against it, or against the God who laid it on her shoulders, not against the poor of Calcutta with whom and for whom she bore it. On the contrary, she gradually came to understand its deeper meaning and even willingly embraced it for the sake of her God.

"Do not look for Jesus away from yourselves. He is not out there. He is in you. Keep your lamp burning and you will recognize him," Mother Teresa said.

Mother Teresa continued, "People are hungry for the Word of God that will give peace that will give unity that will give joy. But you cannot give what you don't have. That's why it is necessary to deepen your life in prayer."

There was no need to go abroad, not even across town, to imitate her or to do something significant with their lives. She pointed to the suffering in the hidden Calcutta's all around them, in their own homes and families and neighborhoods, in the blind man down the street or in the unforgiven relative, forgotten behind the wall of a nursing home. These were all Calcuttas-in-miniature.

Give Your Time, not Money

It was not money that Mother Teresa was seeking from others. She did not throw fund-raisers to raise money for the Sisters of Charity. Mother Teresa never asked or expected her hearers to contribute to her work by sending a check. Instead, she suggested that they "come and see" the work of her Sisters, and learn to spend time with the poor and the needy, to give of their heart, and not just their pocketbook. Writing a check was easily done, and easily done with. It allows us to do charity, while keeping at bay the inner tug that urges us to give more of ourselves and our time, rather than our possessions. This was the challenge people faced, as they discovered that the stir of conscience and heart Mother Teresa awakened both frightened and fascinated them at once.

"I long for God. I long to love Him with every drop of life in me."

Beyond whatever material assistance she gave to the poor, she made it a point to, first of all, sit, listen, and comfort. She gave them her undivided attention. She would spend time simply being present with the poor, face-to-face and heart to heart with those who had no one, knowing no amount of blankets or bricks could warm the human heart. No government program could give the gift of presence; only individual hearts. Only the human heart can communicate the heart of God.

Nobel Prize

In 1979, Mother Teresa was awarded the Nobel Peace Prize. She refused the conventional ceremonial banquet given to laureates and asked that the $192,000 funds be given to the poor in India, stating that earthly rewards were important only if they helped her help the world's needy. When Mother Teresa received the prize, she was asked, "What can we do to promote world peace?" She answered, "Go home and love your family."

She remained true to her beliefs. Undeterred by criticism about her firm stand against abortion and divorce, Mother Teresa stated, "No matter who says what, you should accept it with a smile and do your own work."

For more than forty-five years, Mother Theresa ministered the poor, sick, orphaned, and dying while guiding the Missionaries of Charity's expansion, first throughout India and then in other countries. On March 13, 1997, she stepped down from the head of Missionaries of Charity. She died September 5, 1997.

The Strides She Made

All who sought out Mother Teresa during her life, whether rich or poor, brought with them a deep yearning to be accepted, to be wanted, despite their failings. Whether it was a leper, an old man abandoned and dying in a Calcutta sewer, or a troubled princess, they all came with the same pain, and seeking the same reassurance. In our darkest moments, in our own dark night of the soul, we all yearn to know that love has not left us.

Mother Teresa was personally acquainted with popes, presidents, and royalty. She has never hesitated, however, to do the most menial tasks, and one of her themes is the need for humility.

The world today is hungry not only for bread but hungry for love, hungry to be wanted, to be loved. They are hungry to feel the presence of Christ. As a human being, Mother Teresa brought out the shine and radiance within each of us, of what each of us could be, in order to make this world a better place. God had sent her to soften the rude landscape of human suffering.

She urged us not to ignore Jesus' unseen presence wherever our fellow human beings suffer in body and soul. "Try to deepen your understanding of these words, 'Thirst of God.'" For Mother Teresa, the mystery of God's thirst, revealed in Jesus, is at the center of all, and the key to all. God's yearning to "love and be loved" is the supreme force that inspires and directs all his works. Rather than avoiding suffering, she became intimate with it. Rather than heroically trying to overcome death, she focuses her attention on a person's emotional state and sense of meaning in the last moments.

Her name has become a synonym for compassion and goodness, and she has graced our daily lives. Her image has added a note of goodness, making a home for her not only in Calcutta, but in living rooms around the world. She has become an icon, a symbol of things better and nobler, a reminder of how we and our world could be.

Publicity, fame, money, and riches, failed to shake her inner core. Throughout, she remained true to herself and her vocation, which was to help the needy who had lost hope in this world.

At the time of her death, Mother Teresa's Missionaries of Charity had over 4,000 sisters, and an associated brotherhood of three hundred members, including hospices and homes for people with HIV/AIDS, leprosy, and tuberculosis; soup kitchens; children's and family counseling programs; orphanages; and schools. In time, her work grew to span the globe, causing her to become one of the best known and most highly respected women in the world. Mother Teresa found hope among the hopeless, beauty within what most people considered ugly. She found wealth in poverty. The poor of the world clung to Mother Teresa's sari. Rather than avoiding suffering, she became intimate with it. She became a reminder of how much better our world could be, if only we graced ourselves in love.

Valentina Tereshkova

First Woman to Fly Into Space

The first woman to fly to space, Valentina Tereshkova's successful flight showed that women react as well in space as men do and can handle the stresses of space travel as well as men can.

Valentina Vladimirovna Tereshkova was the first woman to enter the space age. Out of more than four hundred applicants and then out of five finalists, she was selected to pilot Vostok 6 on the 16th of June, 1963. She was also the first civilian in space as she was only inducted into the USSR's Air Force as a condition on joining the Cosmonaut Corps.

Birth and Background

Soviet cosmonaut Valentina Tereshkova was born in the Yaroslavl Region of Russia on March 6, 1937. She was the second born of three children and came from humble beginnings. Her father was a tractor driver and her mother worked in a textile plant. Her family lived during difficult times and worked very hard. Tereshkova helped with the work around the house, so she was not able to start school until she was almost ten years old.

In 1953, she left school and began working. When Tereshkova was eighteen years old, she joined her mother and sister and started working at the cotton mill. She continued her education by taking classes at night. She never allowed financial difficulties to prevent her from getting an education. Economic hardships were rampant, yet they did not stop her from pursuing what she wanted to do with her life.

Valentina became interested in parachute jumping at an early age. It was her expertise in parachute jumping that led to her selection as a cosmonaut. Tereshkova was a textile factory assembly worker and an amateur parachutist when she was recruited into the cosmonaut program.

Participating in the Space Program

Under the direction of Soviet premier Nikita Khrushchev, four women were selected to be trained for a special woman-in-space program. After the flight of Yuri Gagarin in 1961, Sergey Korolyov, the chief Soviet rocket engineer, came up with the idea of putting a woman in space. In 1962, Soviet leader Nikita Khrushchev was ready to send a woman to space. He wanted an ordinary Soviet worker to be the first woman in space. Valentina wrote a letter to the Soviet Space Commission asking if she could train to become a cosmonaut. On February 16, 1962, Tereshkova learned that she was going to train to be a cosmonaut. From thousands of applicants, Valentina Tereshkova and four other women were chosen.

Valentina was told to keep her training a secret from her family and friends, so she told her family and friends that she was training for a women's skydiving team. For the next eighteen months, this cotton mill worker trained to become a cosmonaut. Training included weightless flights, isolation tests, centrifuge tests, rocket theory, spacecraft engineering, 120 parachute jumps, and pilot training in MiG-15UTI jet fighters. She was put in an isolation chamber. She made parachute jumps in a spacesuit. She learned to work in weightless conditions in order to prepare for the lack of gravity. The group spent several months in intensive training, which concluded with examinations in November 1962, after which four remaining candidates were commissioned Junior Lieutenants in the Soviet Air Force. Tereshkova, Solovyova, and Ponomaryova were the leading candidates, and a joint mission profile was developed that would see two women launched into space, on solo Vostok flights on consecutive days, in March or April 1963.

Originally, it was intended that Tereshkova would launch first in Vostok 5 while Ponomaryova would follow her into orbit in Vostok 6. However, this flight plan was altered in March 1963. Vostok 5 would now carry a male cosmonaut, Valery Bykovsky, flying the joint mission with a woman aboard Vostok 6 in June 1963. The State Space Commission nominated Tereshkova to pilot Vostok 6 at their meeting on May 21st and this was confirmed by Nikita Khrushchev himself.

On the morning of June 16, 1963, Tereshkova and her backup Solovyova were both dressed in spacesuits and taken to the launch pad by bus. After completing her communication and life support checks, Tereshkova was sealed inside the Vostok. The news was reported: "After a flawless two-hour countdown, Vostok 6 launched faultlessly and Tereshkova became the first woman to fly into space. On June 16, 1963, at 12.30 p.m. Moscow time, a spaceship, Vostok 6, was launched into orbit piloted, for the first time in history, by a woman, a citizen of the Soviet Union, Communist Comrade Valentina Vladimirovna Tereshkova." Her call sign in this flight was Chaika, later commemorated as the name of an asteroid.

The Vostok 5 mission orbited the Earth forty-eight times. The flight lasted 2.95 days (or 70.8 hours). She soon gave her first impression upon viewing the Earth from space: "It is I, Seagull! Everything is fine. I see the horizon, it's a sky blue with a dark strip. How beautiful the Earth is. Everything is well."

In 2004, when asked of her impressions and memory of viewing Earth, she recalled thinking initially that it was extremely large, but after a few orbits taking less than ninety minutes her view changed, seeing our home planet as a small, fragile, but beautiful place.

Although Tereshkova experienced nausea and physical discomfort for much of the flight, she spent almost three days in space. On this mission, she performed various tests on herself to collect data on the female body's reaction to spaceflight. The objectives of the flight were officially announced as continued studies on the effects of spaceflight on the human organism and specifically, to provide a comparative analysis on the effects of spaceflight on a woman.

With a single flight, Valentina logged more flight time than the combined times of all American astronauts who had flown before that date. Tereshkova also maintained a flight log and took photographs of the horizon, which were later used to identify aerosol layers within the atmosphere. She traveled 1.2 million miles. Although she experienced a little motion sickness, Tereshkova's successful flight showed that women react as well in space as men do and can handle the stresses of space travel as well as men can.

Description of Flight

Twenty-six months and four years after Yuri Gagarin became the first man to fly in space, the Soviet Union succeeded in orbiting the first woman in space on a three-day mission. She became the first woman to fly to space for the next nineteen years.

Official status reports mentioned her conducting extensive tests of the spacecraft, monitoring the controls and onboard equipment, and supervising a program of small experiments including the habitation of the capsule, all part of her contribution to the space program. She also had to log the parameters of the life-support system and her condition during the flight.

Almost immediately upon entering orbit, the adulation and excitement of her achievement spread around the world, and though the mission away from her home planet lasted just three short days, her mission on Earth as a goodwill ambassador began.

The Vostok 5 spacecraft was recovered on June 19, 1963, in the Soviet Union. Tereshkova had parachuted from the spacecraft after earth's atmospheric re-entry; she landed about 380 miles northeast of Karaganda, Kazakhstan.

Upon completion of her mission, Tereshkova was honored with the title "Hero of the Soviet Union." She never flew again, but she did become a spokesperson for the Soviet Union.

Remembering Family

Tereshkova was considered a particularly worthy candidate, partly due to her "proletarian" background and because her father, tank leader sergeant Vladimir Tereshkov, was a war hero. He lost his life in the Finnish Winter War during World War II in the Lemetti area of Finnish Karelia. Tereshkova was two years old at the time of her father's death. After her mission, she was asked how the Soviet Union should thank her for her service to the country. Tereshkova asked that the government search for, and publish, the location where her father was killed-in-action. This was done, and a monument was erected at the site in Lemetti, now on the Russian side of the border. Tereshkova has since visited Finland several times, which shows the deep impact the loss of her father had on her. Yet, Tereshkova used that loss to create great advancements for women and to remember her father in an honorable way.

On November 3, 1963, Tereshkova married another cosmonaut Andrian Nikolayev, who also went into space. They had a daughter, Elena Andrionovna, who was born in 1964. Elena, now a doctor in Russia, was the first child born to parents who both went into space. Elena, was a subject of medical interest because she was the first child born to parents who had both been exposed to space.

Later Achievements

Valentina Tereshkova was given the title "Hero of the Soviet Union," received the Order of Lenin, and was honored with the United Nations Gold Medal of Peace. She never flew in space again. Tereshkova went on to graduate from the Zhuykosky Air Force Engineering Academy in 1969. In 1977, she earned a doctorate in engineering. Due to her prominence she was chosen for several political positions: from 1966 to 1974 she was a member of the Supreme Soviet of the Soviet Union, from 1974 to 1989 a member of the Presidium of the Supreme Soviet, and from 1969 to 1991 she was in the Central Committee of the Communist Party. In 1997, she was retired from the air force and the cosmonaut corps by presidential order.

Tereshkova was invited to President Vladimir Putin's residence in Novo-Ogaryovo for the celebration of her seventieth birthday. While there she said that she would like to fly to Mars, even if it meant that it was a one way trip Tereshkova received the Order of Friendship from Russian President Dmitry Medvedev on April 12, 2011, at the Moscow Kremlin.

The Strides She Made

The Soviet Union did not send another woman into space until nineteen years after her flight. On June 18, 1983, Sally Ride became the first American woman to go to space. It was Tereshkova's brave first flight that paved the way for women of future generations to travel to space. Tereshkova's courage to do something that no other woman had done before in venturing into space was admirable. There was no predecessor to tell her what to expect, how it would affect her body, whether she could bear children after going to space, or if she could withstand the various stress levels. She had the adventurous spirit to venture into the unknown. She was ahead of her time.

Harriet Tubman

Freeing Slaves in the Underground Railway

The Black people called her "Moses."
White plantation owners, however, called
her Harriet "Trouble." Harriet Tubman freed
slaves along the Underground Railway.

- Born into slavery around 1820, in Maryland
- Started working in cotton fields at age four
- Freed slaves along the Underground Railway
- Died in 1913

Harriet Tubman grew up like a neglected weed, ignorant of liberty and having no experience of it. Yet, she always dreamed of freedom and knew that no one would bring it to her unless she ran after it. She escaped the chains of slavery by leaving the plantation she was bound to and using the Underground Railway. She then returned to free hundreds more slaves. In the process, she risked her own life, saying "I can't die but once." She was the conductor of the Underground Railroad for eight years. Tubman became a symbol of hope, courage, and freedom for the slaves.

Harriet Tubman was also a skilled military leader, a compassionate nurse, a committed Abolitionist, and a woman who cared very much about other human beings. Her journey towards freedom began when she tasted a lump of sugar for the first time in her life at age seven.

Background to Slavery

As early as the sixteenth century, African and European slave traders began stealing people from Africa to do heavy labor in the European colonies around the world. Thousands of men, women, and children had been kidnapped from their homes in Africa. The first slaves in the British colonies of North America arrived on a Dutch ship and were sold at Jamestown, Virginia, in 1619. They were sold on the auction block to the highest bidder. The men who sold Africans as slaves became very wealthy. Millions of African Americans consequently were born into slavery in America. They were enslaved in the South and often worked under very harsh conditions. The only release was escape, but few found the courage. This trend continued until President Abraham Lincoln officially freed the slaves in the southern states in 1863.

Birth and Family Background

Harriet Tubman was born into slavery circa 1820. She was one of eleven children born to Harriet Green and Benjamin Ross, slaves on the Edward Brodas plantation on Maryland's eastern shore. She grew up in a small cabin in the slave quarters. Her grandparents were both West Africans who had been captured by slave traders and brought to America in chains.

As soon as Harriet was old enough to pinch cotton, she was forced to work long, hard days. To bring in extra cash, Brodas, her slave master, rented little Harriet to nearby plantations, to people who were nearly as mean as he was. Brodas "rented" her to the Cooks, a poor White couple who couldn't afford to own a slave outright. Harriet was torn from her home. At the Cooks, Harriet slept on the floor in the kitchen near the fireplace and shared scraps of food with the dogs. Mrs. Cook, a weaver, made Harriet spend endless hours in a dusty, dark room, making cloth. Mr. Cook forced the little girl, dressed only in a thin short, to wade daily in the shallows of an ice-cold river to check his muskrat traps. It left her with a vicious cough and fever. Harriet became very sick. The Cooks sent her back to the Brodas plantation only when she was close to death. Master Brodas was a man of little sympathy. As soon as Harriet's cough cleared up, he rented her out again, to a woman who needed a caretaker for her baby.

Tubman remembers one of her slave experiences: "I was only seven years old when I was sent away to take care of a baby. And that baby was always on my lap except when it was asleep or when its mother was feeding it. One morning, after breakfast she had the baby, and I stood by the table waiting, until I was to take it; near me was a bowl of lumps of white sugar. My mistress got into a great quarrel with her husband. She had an awful temper... That sugar... did look so nice, and my mistress's back was turned to me while she was fighting with her husband, so I just put my fingers in the sugar bowl to take one lump and maybe she heard me for she turned and saw me. The next minute she had the rawhide down. I gave one jump out of the door and I saw that they came after me, but I just flew and they didn't catch me."

While running from her mistress, Harriet caught a glimpse of freedom for the first time. Though it was brief, that freedom tasted sweeter than a hundred lumps of sugar. It was something she craved more than anything and it was one of those moments she had created for herself, despite the danger that awaited her, and it felt divine. After a few days, nearly starved, she returned to her mistress, who whipped her.

> "By and by when I was almost tuckered out I came to a great big pigpen. There was an old sow there, and perhaps eight or ten little pigs. I tumbled over and fell in, so beaten out that I could not stir. And there I stayed from Friday until the next Tuesday, fighting

with those little pigs for the potato peelings and other scraps that came down in the trough. The old sow would push me away when I tried to get her children's food, and I was awfully afraid of her. By Tuesday I was so starved I knew I had to go back to my mistress. I didn't have anywhere else to go, even though I knew what was coming. So I went back."

Marriage and Escaping Slavery

In 1844, Harriet married John Tubman, a Black man who had been born free and who had never suffered under the heavy hand of slavery. Though married to a free man, Harriet was, by law, still enslaved. John moved to the Brodas plantation to live with Harriet. John treated Harriet as if she were his slave, doing all he could to stifle Harriet's independence. Whenever Harriet spoke of escaping, John swore he would be among the first to tell the master on her if she fled. Harriet kept quiet. She received little solace or comfort from her husband. John only tried to crush her freedom spirit, which she fought hard to keep from dying completely. Despite living with an abusive husband, Harriet would quietly muster up the courage to believe in herself and seek freedom. This was probably one of the toughest decisions she would ever make in her life.

Harriet knew that escaping from slavery was dangerous. She had heard all kinds of stories about those who tried to flee to the North. The ones who got caught suffered horsewhip beatings or worse. Some were sold away from their parents, wives, and children. Despite the risk of getting caught, Harriet dreamt of freedom.

"Every great dream begins with a dreamer. Always remember, you have within you the strength, the patience, and the passion to reach for the stars to change the world."

Without telling her husband, Harriet gathered three of her brothers and urged them to escape with her. Harriet's brothers agreed, but, as they followed her, their fear of getting caught became too big. Harriet did her best to persuade them to keep on, but all three refused. They made Harriet return to the Brodas plantation. Harriet relented. She vowed to herself that next time she would flee alone. She would flee to the North, where the anti-slavery movement was strong.

Typically, it was men at the time who sought the courage to escape slavery. It was unusual, therefore, for a woman to instill courage on her male family members to seek freedom. Harriet showed more courage than her brothers.

As a woman, she was better at managing change and appeasing conflict, even if it was inside her own mind.

Slaves Down South

In 1849, bad news came to the slaves on the Brodas plantation. The plantation had collected a heap of unpaid bills and the master was planning to pay off his debts by selling some of his slaves. Two of Harriet's sisters were among the first to be sold. They were chained and sent farther south, to Georgia, Mississippi, and Alabama. The life of a slave on a cotton plantation in the Deep South states was often much more harsh than in the states of Maryland, Kentucky, and Virginia. To be sold South was seen as a fate as terrible as death.

Two days later Harriet learned that she had been sold to cotton country and would be chained and sent off the very next day. She realized: "There was one of two things I had a right to, liberty or death; if I couldn't have one, I would have the other."

Underground Railroad

Harriet now ached for freedom more than ever. She had heard of the Abolitionists who sought to end slavery. These people had created a system for hiding runaway slaves who were heading north. The Abolitionists called their hide-and-help system the "Underground Railroad," a network of people willing to hide runaway slaves in their homes...risking their own safety to help slaves get to the North and to freedom. Some of these people were Quakers. Firm in their belief that slavery was wrong, the Quakers opened their homes to hundreds of slaves.

Harriet wanted to go to places she had never been before. To do that, she had to do and act in ways she had never done before. Harriet was a decision-maker. She never wavered or ran away from creating change in her life. Finally, she made the radical decision to leave her husband and the plantation.

One night Harriet wrapped a salted slab of fish and a chunk of bread. She ran and headed toward Bucktown, where a White woman who was helping escaped slaves lived. The woman welcomed her and that night the woman's husband tucked Harriet under a blanket in the bed of his wagon and drove Harriet towards freedom. This was Harriet's first ride on the Underground Railroad. It was a ride she would never forget.

In the morning, the man showed Harriet how to make the rest of her trip on foot, traveling by night and hiding during the day. She feared nothing; not the darkness, not the torrential rains, not the wild animals. The desire for freedom was far greater. Harriet hiked through ninety miles of swamp and woodland. Finally, she found herself north of the Mason-Dixon Line, the boundary between Pennsylvania and Maryland. The Mason-Dixon line became known as the border between the slave states of the South and the free states of the North.

On a morning in 1849, Harriet was free. She said of freedom: "I looked at my hands to see if I was the same person. There was such a glory over everything. The sun came up like gold through the trees, and I felt like I was in heaven."

"I had crossed the line. I was free; but there was no one to welcome me to the land of freedom. I was a stranger in a strange land."

Harriet got herself a job cooking and scrubbing dishes in a hotel kitchen. The work days were long, but Harriet did not mind. She was earning money. She knew that earning money was the first step to becoming independent as a woman.

One night Harriet got word that her sister, Mary, was to be auctioned and sold into cotton country. Working her way from one Underground Railroad station to the next, Harriet guided her kin to Philadelphia, to the freedom she had found. The rescue of her sister encouraged Harriet to go back to slave country again, to bring the rest of her family to the North. Risking her life, she returned to the South many times to help hundreds of other slaves who were not afraid to flee.

Harriet Tubman wanted to share the happiness that she had of freedom with others. Rather than keeping it all to herself, she wanted to light the lives of other slaves who ached in their shackles. Her greatness lay in her fearlessness to embrace danger rather than running away from it.

In 1851, on her third trip, Harriet returned to the Brodas plantation to get her husband, John. Harriet hoped that John Tubman had changed his ways and would come with her to Pennsylvania. She knocked on his door. John opened it. He had a new wife. He met her with a smirk and told her he wasn't going anywhere. Harriet left the plantation and never looked back. She never saw her husband again and she rarely spoke about him.

Moses

Harriet now traveled twice a year. The Black people called her "Moses." White plantation owners, however, called Harriet "Trouble." Runaway slaves were advertised on handbills and on leaflets that included a picture and description of the slave. The authorities severely punished people who helped slaves escape.

By 1854, Tubman was well known throughout the Eastern Shore. The authorities offered a $12,000 reward for Tubman's capture...a reward for anyone who captured "the woman called 'Moses.' Bounty hunters often searched for her. If Harriet Tubman was ever afraid during these dangerous trips, she did not show it. She believed very strongly in what she was doing to help other Black people.

In 1857, she made one of her most meaningful escape missions — she finally rescued her parents. Because her parents had grown elderly and were too old to travel on foot, Harriet had been waiting for just the right time to take them to freedom. One night she broke into a stable on the Brodas plantation, hitched a horse to a wagon, hid her parents in the back of the wagon, and dashed off.

Harriet Tubman had made the journey North some nineteen times. She led as many as three hundred slaves to freedom. Each trip was different, but Tubman was never caught. She said of her trips: "I never ran my train off the track, and I never lost a passenger."

"If I could have convinced more slaves that they were slaves, I could have freed thousands more."

Tubman During the Civil War

On January 1, 1863, President Abraham Lincoln issued the Emancipation Proclamation, a document that called for the freedom of all slaves. There was no further need for the Underground Railroad. Black people could travel freely anywhere they wished.

During the Civil War, Harriet Tubman served as a nurse for the Union soldiers. She also spied for the North by collecting information from African Americans living in Confederate Territory. After the war, she supported orphans and old people and worked to give African Americans the education she never had.

Financial Shackles

Tubman experienced continuous money problems. She had carefully saved her receipts and records from the war years and, using these documents, Tubman asked her friends to help her figure out how much money the U.S. government owed her. They calculated that the government owed her $1,800 for her military services. Tubman desperately needed the money to support herself, her parents, and others who were very poor. Congress refused to recognize the rights of this Black woman who had worked so hard and fought so bravely for her country.

When Sarah Bradford published a biography of Tubman called *Scenes in the Life of Harriet Tubman* in 1869, she turned the profits from the book over to Tubman. The $1,200 helped her greatly.

Harriet Tubman never lost a passenger in the Underground Railway. "If I could have convinced more slaves that they were slaves, I could have freed thousands more," she once said.

The Strides She Made

Harriet Tubman died on March 10, 1913, at 93 in Auburn, New York. Today, Harriet's life continues to inspire women for her courage and independent spirit. She allowed no one to trample her and make her feel she was not worthy. She risked her life to share her taste of freedom. Rather than wasting her daring journeys trying to force freedom on people who did not want it, like her husband, she invested her efforts in people who longed to have freedom, but were afraid to get it on their own. Harriet Tubman became that "crutch" that many slaves at the time, needed to find freedom.

"Every great dream begins with a dreamer. Always remember, you have within you the strength, the patience, and the passion to reach for the stars to change the world."

Madam C. J. Walker

First Woman Millionaire by her Own Achievements

Walker used her wealth as a means to further
her political activism and philanthropic work.
Photo courtesy www.madamcjwalker.com.

- Born on December 23, 1867, in Louisiana, to slave parents

- Orphaned at seven, married at fourteen, and widowed at twenty

- Spent years laboring as a washerwoman for $1.50 a week

- Made her fortune by developing and marketing a successful line of beauty and hair products

- Active philanthropist and political activist for the African American community

- Died on May 25, 1919

A family is sometimes blessed with one child whose imagination can expand beyond familiar expectations and who rises to an unimaginable level of success. Madam C.J. Walker was that child who broke away from the shackles that trapped her parents in slavery and poverty and rose to unimaginable prosperity. She was like a cactus blooming in a vast desert of emotional hardships and emotional loss, yet, not allowing those hardships to crush her spirits. Nor did she allow other people to determine the limits of her life. If she did, Madam C.J. Walker would never have grown into the woman that she became.

Madam C.J. Walker became hardened by her tragedies and wanted a better life. The girl born Sarah Breedlove became a woman of great reserve and dignity. It is a miraculous transformation from obscurity and poverty to wealth. She developed a cosmetic line that defined the face of African America beauty. She used her wealth as a means to further her political activism and philanthropic work. She sought opportunities and never waited for opportunity to knock at her door. She strove, she sought, and finally she found it.

She was born into poverty in a cotton plantation in the Mississippi and died as the first female African American millionaire. And it was all sparked by a dream...

Birth and Background

Her name when she was born was Sarah Breedlove. On her tombstone she is called Madam C.J. Walker. She was born in poverty-stricken rural Delta, Louisiana, on December 23, 1867. Her place of birth is described as "Grand View, Robert W.Burney's thousand acre plantation overlooking the Mississippi." Her parents and elder siblings were slaves on a plantation owned by Robert W. Burney. This farm was a battle-staging area during the Civil War for General Ulysses S. Grant and his Union troops.

Walker was born in poverty-stricken rural Delta, Louisiana, on December 23, 1867.
Photo courtesy www.madamcjwalker.com.

Sarah Breedlove's parents were croppers. When Sarah was a baby her mother either strapped her to her back while she worked in the fields, or sat her on a long burlap bag and pulled her along the rows, keeping a sharp eye out for copperheads and moccasins.

By the age of four a cropper's child had a job drilling holes for cotton seeds and dropping them in carefully. Sarah became one of the best pickers. Having an early childhood filled with physical hardships had a good side to it. It gave her an excellent work ethic and tolerance for hard work. Sarah never complained about working hard and this trait would become her stamp for success in her later years.

> *"There is no royal flower strewn path to success. And if there is, I have not found it; for if I have accomplished anything in life it is because I have been willing to work hard."*

Her mother, Minerva Breedlove, died in 1872. If the disease that killed her was swamp fever or malaria, it might have been in her system for a year or longer, leaving her sporadically achy and exhausted. Sarah Breedlove lay at her dying mother's feet. Her father remarried and died shortly afterwards. By age seven, she was an orphan. Sarah and her older sister survived by working in the cotton fields. Soon, she moved in with her older sister and brother-in-law, Willie Powell, across the river to Vicksburg in 1878 to obtain work. She was ten.

A Millionaire Among Washerwomen

Sarah's first two years in Vicksburg were spent as a washerwoman. On Mondays she went to pick up laundry, walking through muddy streets and hills to get to different homes. Early on, she developed a high tolerance for physical pain.

After bringing the dirty laundry back, all the other women in the shacks adjoining hers, gathered and did the washing. On Saturday she delivered the laundry clean, starched, ironed, and folded.

It was at the washing place that the seeds for big ideas began to brew. Young Sarah took note of every detail. Some women learned how to make soap from fat drippings and wood ashes. Most women added lye to the mixture, which burnt their arms. If the proportion of ashes to grease was not exactly right, homemade soap stained clothes or turned them yellow. When they could afford it, laundresses made deals with the soap cart driver, buying ready made cakes at a discount, in exchange for drippings they had collected. Sarah observed the importance of heat in the entire laundering process: making soap, cleaning clothes, starching, and ironing. Her mind was clicking.

Even in the most mundane of activities, whether it was washing clothes or picking up soiled linen, Sarah's mind was thinking of ways to do something great. While other women gossiped and confined their minds to washing clothes, Sarah let her mind wander to faraway places. Sarah thought big.

Marriage and Motherhood

Sarah married Moses McWilliams when she was fourteen years old to get a home of her own and to escape her sister's husband's abuse. Marriage was an escape. On June 6, 1885, she satisfied one great desire and had a baby. Sarah named her baby Lelia McWilliams or A'Lelia Walker. When Sarah was twenty and her daughter had just turned two, Moses, her husband died.

Thus far, Louisiana was the territory that was familiar to her. In order to remove herself of any memories of the tragedies she had endured until this point, and also to seek greater things, Sarah decided to venture into the unknown. In about 1887 she moved with her daughter to St. Louis, Missouri. She had three brothers who worked as barbers there.

From her train seat, Sarah saw the two places she had spent her entire life thus far: the flat swamps of Delta and the Red Bluffs of Vicksburg. At the age of twenty, Sarah had the strength to make decisive changes in her life. Relief trumped fear. Anticipation removed exhaustion. Her desire for success was larger than her fear of failure. Sarah didn't expect St. Louis to be paradise, but she believed that life will be better there, especially for her daughter. She wanted something better for herself and her daughter, and to seek that, she had to get out of her comfort zone.

Sarah's second marriage to John Davis took place on August 11, 1894. It failed and ended sometime in 1903. In 1905, Sarah's brother died. In July 1905, with $1.50 in savings, the 37-year-old moved to Denver where she joined her deceased brother's wife and four daughters.

Sarah married for the third time in January 1906, to Charles Joseph "C.J." Walker, a newspaperman with an innate ability for marketing. Sarah now changed her name to Madam C.J. Walker.

Scalp Disease

Sarah was losing some of her hair. She had been having trouble with dandruff, dryness, and worst of all, bald spots for at least fifteen years. Several reasons could be attributed. Scalp disease was common at that time, especially among African Americans. Stress and hardship had begun to take their toll on her, which may have impacted her hair falling out. Another was related to the lack of hygienic conditions available to common people at the time. Most homes lacked indoor plumbing, central heating, and electricity. Consequently, they bathed and washed their hair infrequently. The result was scalp disease. Poor diet may have been another cause.

In addition, Sarah was also probably experimenting with concoctions to tame her natural frizz so that she could style it however she wished. Sarah experimented with homemade remedies and developed her own recipes. Most of these substances contained either sulfur or lye, often mixed with capsicum, red pepper, or cayenne — all of which could badly burn the scalp.

In the spring of 1906, Sarah claimed that lightning struck and her life changed overnight. She had a dream: "A big Black man appeared to me and told me what to mix for my hair. He gave me a formula for curing baldness. The Black man told me which herbs and oils I needed. Some of the remedy was grown in Africa, but I sent for it, put it on my scalp, and in a few weeks my hair was coming in faster than it had ever fallen out." Sarah claimed to have built her company and her empire based around this dream.

A dream it may have been, yet her mind at the time was so saturated with hair growing formula that it was no coincidence that she was dreaming about it all day and night. The only way to make her dream real was to wake up and that is exactly what she did. Life would never be the same for this woman who, thus far, had only tasted what it was like to be poor.

Wonderful Hair Grower Formula

Madam C.J. Walker experimented with home remedies and products already on the market until she finally developed her own shampoo and an ointment that contained sulfur to make her scalp healthier for hair growth. After she shared her formula with some friends and found it successful for them as well, she realized that there were almost no hair products available for Blacks.

She founded her own business and began selling her own product called "Madam Walker's Wonderful Hair Grower," a scalp conditioning and healing formula. She also began selling "Glossine" pressing oil and "Vegetable Shampoo" door-to-door and began instructing women on hair and scalp treatments. Her products ranged from hair conditioners and facial creams to hot combs specially made for the hair of Black consumers.

Walker founded her own business and began selling her product called "Madam Walker's Wonderful Hair Grower," a scalp conditioning and healing formula.
Photo courtesy www.madamcjwalker.com.

She worked during the day as a cook in order to finance her part-time business. Her success was immediate. In less than a year, she was doing business of $25 to $35 a week.

Madam C.J. Walker played an important role in laying the foundation for modern hairstyling and straightening trends for African American women, who sought other styles besides the "Afro" look. She gave African American women the "Green" light to create artificial looks for their hair and was bold enough to create a product for African American women that opened new cosmetic trends. Rather than confining to their natural hairstyles, which some were unhappy with, she enabled them to create unique looks that suited their faces and bodies.

"I got my start by giving myself a start," said Walker.

The hair product was controversial for many reasons. Many people felt that African American women should wear their hair in natural styles rather than attempting to change the texture from curly to straight. When confronted with the idea that she was trying to conform Black women's hair to that of whites, Madam C.J. Walker stressed that her products were simply an attempt to help Black women take proper care of their hair and promote its growth. It was not a racial slur that she was trying to create, but rather a beauty slant for African American women. In spite of critics, Walker's hair care methods gained increasing popularity among African American women, who enjoyed products designed especially for them.

Madam C.J. Walker brought haute couture into the home. Now, women did not have to go to the salon every time they wanted their hair straightened. They were able to buy the product and style their hair by themselves at home. "Perseverance is my motto," she said.

Door to Door Consultations

Madam C.J. Walker's marketing strategy was ingenious, as she managed to tap into a female audience who was so desperate to change their lives and their appearances. She capitalized on this and offered a simple product and service that boosted their self esteem. Her cosmetics gave women the boldness to walk out in public in style. Through her cosmetic line, she reminded African American women how beautiful they looked and allowed them to take pride in themselves rather than feel ashamed.

Neither a marketing degree from a university nor any coaching from a business savvy parent guided Madam C.J. Walker to come up with her marketing strategy. Tapping into her own creative mind and using her strong work ethic as her foundation, she went door to door, selling her hair products. Her early days of canvassing neighborhoods to pick up dirty laundry and deliver clean ones certainly helped her to master the art of knocking on strange doors, one household at a time. The full-out push began. "Imagine, prepare, go out and get it," she said.

Most people thought the secret ingredient that was curing baldness in her products was sulfur, and not until almost a hundred years later will descendants of Madam C.J. Walker affirm that, indeed, precipitated sulfur was a major ingredient in the recipe. While methods have changed, the basic idea remains the same even today.

In September 1906, Madam C.J. Walker and her husband promoted their products and training sales agents. They recruited people to sell her products. They settled in Pittsburgh in 1908 and opened Lelia College to train "hair culturists." They also formed the "Madam C.J. Walker Manufacturing Company." Madam C.J. Walker began placing advertisements in Black newspapers throughout the United States. Soon, she was selling her products throughout the country. While her daughter Lelia ran a mail-order business from Denver, Madam C.J. Walker and her husband traveled throughout the southern and eastern states.

In 1910, Madam Walker moved to Indianapolis, Indiana, where she established her headquarters. Indianapolis was then the country's largest inland manufacturing base. The access to eight major railway systems helped Walker greatly in her distribution of her products. She called the company "The Walker College of Hair Culture and Walker Manufacturing Co."

Although she divorced in 1912, Madam C.J. Walker learned a lot of marketing techniques from her third husband. He stayed on as a sales agent for the company. "When we began to make $10 a day, my husband thought that was enough, thought I ought to be satisfied, but I was convinced that my hair preparation would fill a long felt want. And when we found it impossible to agree, due to his narrowness of vision, I embarked on business for myself."

Establishing Walker Agents

By 1919, Madam C.J. Walker employed several dozen people working at the factory and had more than 3,000 "Walker Agents" marketing her cosmetic products. Newspaper and magazine ads solicited women to become selling agents, with a promise of guaranteed weekly salaries.

The woman who was earlier living in a St. Louis tenement, now had a large, brick house with three porches and a telephone. It was during this time that Walker expanded her company internationally to Jamaica, Cuba, Costa Rica, Panama, and Haiti. Madam C.J. Walker's "Walker System," which included a broad offering of cosmetics, licensed Walker Agents, and Walker Schools offered meaningful employment and personal growth to Black women. She used her money to make a difference in the lives of African Americans by offering them jobs.

Madam Walker was quite the businesswoman. Soon, her company grew beyond anyone's expectations. By 1917, she incorporated her set up instructions into a formal, oft quoted and very forceful policy statement. She created a listing of Hints to Agents:

- Keep yourself clean as well as your parlor or room in which you do your work. The room should be cleaned thoroughly before beginning your work every morning. Open your windows. Air it well. When the room is not in use even in winter, throw up the windows, it will drive out germs.
- Keep a waste basket in your parlor and after each customer clean up the hair and matches from the floor.
- Cleanse and sterilize the comb and sponge after each customer. It would be well to keep such things on hand that each customer might purchase as his own.
- Keep your teeth clean in order that the breath might be sweet. Five cents of mints will last a week. Put one in the mouth before beginning a customer. If her breath is offensive, offer her one.
- See that your fingernails are kept clean, as that is a mark of refinement.
- See that your hair always looks well. In order to interest others you must first make the impression by keeping your hair in first class condition.
- Do not be narrow and selfish to the extent that you would not sell goods to anybody because they do not take the treatment from you. We are anxious to help all humanity, the poor as well as the rich, especially those of our race. There are thousands who would buy and use the goods who are not able to pay the extra cost of having it done for them. The hair may not grow as rapidly nor look as beautiful, but they will get results, as long as they are satisfied and you have made your profit from the sale, all is well.

Madam C.J. Walker also gave each agent specific agent instructions on representing her company:

"Acquaint yourself with the history and life of Madam C.J. Walker, get on the very tip of your tongue the strong points that you will find in the story of her personal experience, tell your prospective customer about her, do so in an intelligent and emphatic way, watch his or her face, watch what statement impresses the most, and then drive the nail home. Make every moment count; when you make a call remember that you are there to make a sale and also a customer for the company. Be tactful, if you find that one line of talk won't work, try another, Always remembering that you are there to sell."

Revolutionary Business Module

Madam Walker used a revolutionary business model of door-to-door canvassing, training sales agents, and traveling cross-country to promote her products. She revolutionized the way business was done, especially for the African American entrepreneurial community. She traveled throughout the nation demonstrating her products, recruiting salespersons, and encouraging African American entrepreneurs to start their own businesses. She organized conventions of African American organizations, churches, and civic groups. She held gatherings where agents were tutored in product use, hygienic care techniques, and marketing strategies. She also gave cash awards to those who were most successful in promoting sales.

African American women loved her products. This resulted in growing profits for Walker's business and an increasing number of agents who marketed the products for her door-to-door.

Offering Women Jobs

Madam C.J. Walker understood that many women were enslaved by their husbands and families because of financial reasons. The solution was simple: just give them a job. And that is exactly what she did. She used her wealth for improving the lives of the poor.

She actively recruited women, thus creating financial independence in their lives. She gave them a way of rising above the constraints set by a male dominated society. Through her business module, she empowered women so that they would not have to remain in abusive situations because of their financial dependence on men. Years earlier, she had married at fourteen in order to escape her sister's abusive husband. She hoped her own husband would be able to provide for her financially. That never happened. Now that she had the financial potential, she wanted to create a better life for other women trapped in similar situations.

*"I am not satisfied in making money for myself.
I endeavor to provide employment
for hundreds of the women of my race."*

Philanthropic and Social Work

Madam C.J. Walker used her wealth as a springboard to advance her philanthropic and political activism. For her, money was a means to making a difference in society, especially for the people of her race. Rather than amassing wealth for fame and glory, she used money to make a difference for the majority. Her happiness was to share her new-found wealth rather than hoarding it for her own glory.

Madam C.J. Walker was a philanthropist. In 1918, at the biennial convention of the National Association of Colored Women (NACW), she was acknowledged for making the largest contribution to save the Anacostia (Washington, DC) house of Abolitionist Frederick Douglass. She continued to donate money throughout her career to the NACW, the YMCA, and to Black schools, organizations, individuals, orphanages, and retirement homes.

Madam C.J. Walker became an inspiration to many Black women. Fully recognizing the power of her wealth and success, she lectured to promote her business, which, in turn, empowered other women in business. She gave lectures on Black issues at conventions sponsored by powerful Black institutions. She also encouraged Black Americans to support the cause of World War I and worked to have Black veterans granted full respect.

> "I am a woman who came from the cotton fields of the South. From there I was promoted to the washtub. From there I was promoted to the cook kitchen. And from there I promoted myself into the business of manufacturing hair goods and preparations. I have built my own factory on my own ground."

Embracing Her Past and Living the High Life

Madam C.J. Walker was constantly on a quest for learning new things. She never let up in her pursuit of the two things she valued most: respectability and education. Believing that if she focused on the latter, the former would follow, she hired women to teach her vocabulary, to correct her grammar, and broaden her horizons. In the mornings she demanded serious readings of the newspaper, and if a word nobody knew came up, somebody had to go look up it up in the dictionary then and there.

Throughout her rise to wealth, she embraced her past, without feeling ashamed about it. This made her embrace her life and her humble beginnings. At the 13th Annual Convention of the National Negro Business League in August 1912, she said, "I am not ashamed of my past. I am not ashamed of my humble beginnings. Don't think because you have to go down in the wash tub you are any less a lady!"

Talking to the New York Times in 1917, Madam C.J. Walker confesses to having a few interests beyond her obsession with business: The advancement of her race, music, cars, and sports.

Walker is the first African American woman to become a self-made millionaire. *Photo courtesy www.madamcjwalker.com.*

In 1917, she moved to her Irvington on Hudson, New York, estate, Villa Lewaro, which had been designed by Vertner Tandy, the first licensed Black architect in New York State and a founding member of Alpha Phi Alpha Fraternity. The house cost $250,000 to build. It was a 34-room mansion built off of the Hudson River in New York. Her neighbors included industrialists Jay Gould and John D. Rockefeller. The grand estate served not only as her home, but also as a meeting place for summits of race leaders to discuss current issues.

First African American Woman to Become a Millionaire

Madam C.J. Walker's aggressive marketing strategy combined with relentless ambition led her to be labeled as the first known African American woman to become a self made millionaire. Having amassed a fortune in fifteen years, at her death she was considered to be the wealthiest African American woman in America. Some sources cite her as the first self made American woman millionaire.

Madam C.J. Walker is a woman remembered by who she became: a product, an icon, a legend, and an exemplar. Her leadership and fame, particularly in light of the barriers of race, gender, and literacy are awe-inspiring, especially considering the mind-set of the South. Her prescription for success was perseverance, hard work, faith in herself and in God, honest business dealings,

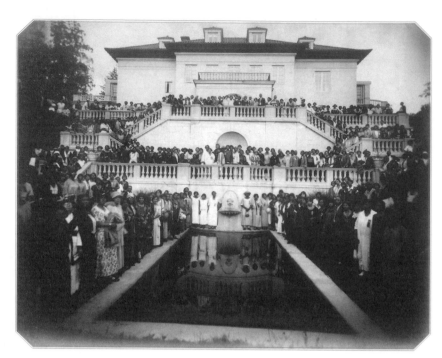

In 1917, Madam C.J. Walker moved to her Irvington on Hudson, New York, estate, Villa Lewaro. It was a 34-room mansion built off of the Hudson River in New York. Her neighbors included industrialists Jay Gould and John D. Rockefeller. *Photo courtesy www.madamcjwalker.com.*

and quality products. She advises other women with dreams of making it in the business world: "I had to make my own living and my own opportunity, but I made it! Don't sit down and wait for the opportunities to come. Get up and make them."

Madam C.J. Walker died at Villa Lewaro on Sunday, May 25, 1919, from complications of hypertension. She was fifty-one. Her daughter, A'Lelia Walker, became the president of the C.J Walker Manufacturing Company. She is buried in the Bronx in the Woodlawn Cemetery, not far from the much grander digs of J.C. Penney and F.W. Woolworth. Minerva Breedlove, a slave, would never have dreamt that one of her daughters would be buried adjacent to the biggest retail moguls in the world.

The Strides She Made

Madam C.J. Walker revolutionized the hair care and cosmetics industry for African American women early in the twentieth century. Her discovery created a revolutionary hair care formula for Black women and everything changed for them. If they were dissatisfied with how their hair looked, she gave them the option of doing something about it. If they were bald and had lost hopes of marriage or were being teased, they could now do something about it.

Madam C.J. Walker boosted the self esteem of African American women by helping them to feel beautiful about themselves through her cosmetic products. She gave them self confidence to change their predicament if it ostracized them in an image conscious society. She encouraged women to experiment with their looks and to come up with hairstyles that suited their individuality, thus encouraging them to take pride in an individual look rather than the conformities that society had harshly imposed upon them. Beauty was something she delivered, one woman at a time. It was not like an assembly line of women waiting to look the same, but rather, the contours and aesthetics of every woman were accentuated, leaving them feeling special about themselves. Every woman who tried her cosmetic product was made to feel, "Yes, I am beautiful," and that is all that mattered.

The value of her life is more multidimensional than the beauty and cosmetic aspects. Her role as a philanthropist and political activist is in many ways what made her stand out to the larger Black community. The sale of hair care products provided the means to an end.

Oprah Winfrey

Media Queen

- Born in Mississippi in 1954
- Talk show host of "The Oprah Winfrey Show"
- Owns a media empire
- African American billionaire of her own achievements
- One of the most influential women and powerful personalities in the world

From farmhouse to penthouse, from a life of struggles to a life of riches, from playing with a corncob doll to becoming one of the first female billionaires of the world, Oprah Winfrey's story to fame and fortune is truly an amazing one. She has shaken the world in every imaginable field — in media, education, fashion, food, health, business, philanthropy, medicine, and more — with the so-called "Oprah Effect" creating thousands of successful people, almost like creating an offspring of mini-Oprahs all over the world. She has become one of the most successful, influential, and powerful personalities of our times: a host, actor, publisher, and the creator of a cable network. Through it all, Oprah has launched thousands of careers.

Oprah was wired for success. Yet, the wiring came only after a firing. From the point of losing her broadcasting job, she created her own future of success. Nothing could stop her from becoming one of the most influential women of our time.

Birth and Farm Life in Mississippi

Born on January 29, 1954, in Mississippi, Oprah was the great-great-granddaughter of slaves. In Mississippi at the time, in the area where she was growing up, segregation colored the lives of African Americans. Oprah could not escape the effects of slavery and the attitude that society imposed upon her.

Oprah lived in a farmhouse which had some of the basic facilities. It was a small farm with a few animals. There was no indoor plumbing. To get to the farm from town, visitors had to come up a dusty, unpaved road. It was a lonely location, yet, there was plenty to do around the farm. The nearest neighbor was an elderly blind man. Her one and favorite toy doll was a doll that had been fashioned from a corncob.

Chores kept her busy. There was plenty to eat, with all of it being grown on the farm. The basic necessities were there, but there was little money to afford some of the other amenities that a little girl would have desired. There were few modern conveniences. While growing up, she had no telephone. Nor was there a television. "I never had a store-bought dress," Oprah remembered later.

Despite her early economic hardships on the farmhouse, Oprah never saw her future as being limited in any way. Though life didn't start out easy for her, even as a child she believed she could do anything if she set her mind to it.

"I don't think of myself as a poor deprived ghetto girl who made good. I think of myself as somebody who from an early age knew I was responsible for myself, and I had to make good."

Oprah began to do recitations in church. For Oprah, public speaking was a way to get attention and love. Early on, she showed a passion for standing in front of people and talking to them.

As an adult, Oprah didn't remember that her mother had lived with her on the farm at all. It seemed as if she had always been gone. Her mother moved to Milwaukee to get a job. With her mother gone, the only woman who counted in Oprah's life was her grandmother, Hattie Mae, who was determined that her granddaughter would use all the gifts and talents that she had. Oprah always tried to make her grandmother proud. It would be safe to assume that during these first six years on the farmhouse, she had developed her inner security, her inner self confidence, and colorful imagination for larger things to come.

When Oprah was only a small child, her grandmother taught her how to read. Reading opened up all kinds of possibilities for her. Many times, Oprah has called reading the foundation of her success. Later on, she would show her respect for reading through the formation of her Book Club, which drew millions of readers and rekindled their love for reading in a computer ridden age. She would also go on to build libraries for underprivileged children, noting, "Books were my pass to personal freedom. I learned to read at age three, and soon discovered there was a whole world to conquer that went beyond our farm in Mississippi."

Oprah's life in Mississippi had a reassuring consistency — church, farmhouse chores, and reading — and then everything changed. By 1959, her mother, Vernita, had gotten herself settled in Milwaukee and she wanted her daughter living there with her. Farm life was over. There would be no more quiet and lonely days telling stories to animals; no more time to spend with her fierce but loving grandmother. Oprah was six when she left Mississippi.

Life in Milwaukee

Now, the six-year-old Oprah lived in a small room in a boardinghouse. Instead of being raised by a grandmother with a watchful eye, Oprah was often left to her own devices while her mother was away cleaning houses in the Milwaukee suburbs. Oprah also had a new baby sister by this time, Patricia. Oprah was soon to learn that the things she had been most prized for in Mississippi — her love of reading and her public speaking abilities — would go unnoticed in her mother's household or, perhaps, her mother was too busy working that she lacked the energy and relaxation to sit with Oprah and appreciate her talents. Oprah's mother was so busy battling economic hardships that keeping a close eye on the little girl was difficult.

Vernita was twenty-four and trying to raise two children was hard. She sent Oprah to her father, Vernon Winfrey, who now had a wife, Zelma. Oprah was excited. She wanted a father as a male figure in her life and also for security. Oprah was enjoying life with her father in a home, but soon her mother took her back.

When Oprah's mother conceived a third child, it was Oprah's responsibility to watch over the two younger siblings. Oprah assumed motherly responsibilities at an early age; while this may have robbed her of her childhood innocence, it prepared her well for adult life. Watching the difficult circumstances under which her mother was raising three children may have also darkened Oprah's early childhood memories of motherhood. Rather than seeing it as something happy and special, she probably absorbed memories of pain, darkness, and suffering of being a mother.

The Joy of School Days

Oprah liked school. "One of the defining moments in my life came in the fourth grade, the year I was Mrs. Duncan's student," she recalls. Mrs. Duncan was one of the positive highlights of her school career. Through a scholarship in Outward Bound, Oprah was able to attend Nicolet High School in 1968. Oprah was well aware of the importance of her African American heritage. She especially admired Harriet Tubman, a runaway slave who, at great personal sacrifice, led hundreds of other slaves to freedom on the Underground Railroad.

Oprah enrolled at Tennessee State University, although college was not much to her liking. While in her senior year, she got a part-time job reading the news at WVOL radio station. Oprah's ongoing job reading the news at WVOL was one of the best parts of her early college years. While still in college, she was offered a job by Chris Clark at WTVF television. Her salary was $15,000 a year — as much as Vernon, her father, was making at the barber shop.

Oprah knew she had a talent, and she was determined to cultivate it and make it blossom to the fullest to make a difference in people's lives. From her childhood, Oprah had a rare and special talent: The ability to communicate with her audience so intimately that it made her seem more like a friend than a broadcaster.

"My greatest gift is my ability to talk, and to be myself at all times, no matter what. I am as comfortable in front of the camera with a million people watching me as I am sitting here talking to you. I have the ability to be perfectly vulnerable at all times."

In 1976, at only twenty-six years old, things were not going too well with Oprah being a newscaster in Baltimore on WJZ-TV. She was removed from her anchor chair and sent out to be a street reporter, frequently covering murders and natural disasters. These assignments were not to her liking. Oprah knew that soon she was about to be fired. This did not dissuade her from a career in public speaking. She did not give up.

"Do the one thing you think you cannot do. Fail at it. Try again. Do better the second time. The only people who never tumble are those who never mount the high wire. This is your moment. Own it."

Suddenly, something unexpected happened. WJZ-TV was planning a new program, an interview show called *People are Talking*. Oprah was named the co-host. By the time the first show was over, she realized the immediate effect it had made on her life. Later, she would go on to say, "I came off of that stage August 14, 1978, and I knew that I was home. In all my years of being discontent, feeling like something's not quite right, feeling like I was in the wrong place, in the wrong job, I knew this is it. It felt like home because it felt so natural. It felt like I could be myself."

Oprah Winfrey was now a talk show host and the world of television would never quite be the same again.

Through talent, drive, ambition, and a profound sense of self, Oprah turned what seemed to be her biggest drawbacks: her status as an "other" and a pariah, into assets. She approached topics from a different angle. She projected qualities that mere experience could not generate: empathy, curiosity, energy, and passion.

"Be thankful for what you have; you'll end up having more. If you concentrate on what you don't have, you will never, ever have enough."

Starting the Oprah Winfrey Show

"My first day in Chicago, September 4, 1983, I set foot in this city, and just walking down the street, it was like roots, like the motherland. I knew I belonged here." She was offered a job for $200,000 a year. Oprah starred as the host of *A.M. Chicago* on January 2, 1984. In January 1985, *A.M. Chicago* was lengthened to an hour and renamed *The Oprah Winfrey Show*.

While Oprah's fame is largely attributed to *The Oprah Winfrey Show*, she was also an actress. She auditioned for a role in *The Color Purple*, by Alice Walker. Director Steven Spielberg personally called her and said she got the part. Her role in the film was Sofia, a betrayed and battered woman. When the Oscar Nominations were announced in early 1986, *The Color Purple* was nominated for eleven awards. One of those nominations went to Oprah Winfrey for "Best Supporting Actress."

"My philosophy is that not only are you responsible for your life, but doing the best at this moment puts you in the best place for the next moment."

Whatever she did, Oprah gave it two hundred percent. Excellence was her trademark and she was determined to do her best. She was aware of her racial identity, but did not feel burdened by it. Rather, she embraced it because she understood that being Black was who she was. "Excellence is the best deterrent to racism or sexism," Oprah has said.

Programs on controversial topics gave *The Oprah Winfrey Show* an edge. It gave credibility in the eyes of viewers and brought more visibility and influence to Oprah personally. She covered weight loss issues, sexual molestation, pornography, homosexuality, and other edgy and taboo topics.

Certainly, when she made her leap from local talk show to national syndication in 1986, no one was expecting much more than modest success. Entering a television landscape dominated by some big media names at the time, she was the reverse image of the supposed ideal host: female instead of male, Black instead of White, large instead of petite. She would overtake all of them and become one of the biggest media moguls of our time.

"The greatest discovery of all time is that a person can change his future by merely changing his attitude."

Media Mogul

After the seedling years of 1984-1986, Oprah burst into full bloom. She was in complete control of her public image and became a gigantic mogul. She had her own media empire: her own television network, her own radio show, her own website, her own daily talk show, and her own magazine. She flowered as a national success at the age of thirty-two and the money rained down in torrents. She was television's highest paid talk show host.

Once Oprah became a millionaire, she announced that she was going to become "the richest Black woman in the world."

"No one makes it alone. Everyone who has achieved any level of success in life was able to do so because something or someone served as a beacon to light the way. What seems to be an endless cycle of generational poverty and despair can be broken if each of us is willing to be a light to the other. When you learn, teach. When you get, give. That is how you change the world: one life, one family at a time."

Most people were genuinely delighted by Oprah's success and inspired by her gospel: "If I can do it, you can do it." She was heralded for personifying the American Dream with all its honeyed promise of equal opportunity She encouraged her fans and followers to find their own stage in this world, whether it be as a single woman, a mother, a Fortune 500 Company CEO, a janitor, or a school teacher.

Throughout her career, Oprah has won seven Daytime Emmys for Outstanding Talk Show, seven NAACP Image awards, Broadcaster of the Year from the International Radio and Television Society, a Lifetime Achievement Award from the Academy of Television Arts and Sciences, and many more.

When Oprah appeared on the *Forbes* list of the world's 476 billionaires in February 2003, she became what she had set out to be: The richest Black woman in the world. However, she has said of her newfound wealth: "What material success does is provide you with the ability to concentrate on other things that really matter. And that is being able to make a difference, not only in your own life, but in other people's lives."

The Strides She Made

Oprah Winfrey is one of the most influential people in America. She is a well-known cultural and financial icon of our time who has touched the lives of millions all over the world — girls, boys, men, and women alike. She exploited the power of television and how it could transform lives. Oprah also created a generation of entrepreneurs. "The Oprah Effect" is the explosive effects of her influence. Her impact on business is worth billions. Oprah has turned "no-names" into brand names.

Oprah also exposed topics that other talk show hosts dreaded to expose. She became the public confidante to millions of women who had been raped, molested, and abused. Oprah gave them the courage to stand up and walk away from abusive situations. She became a friend to men who had been molested by their fathers, uncles, priests, and neighbors. She shone their inner beauty and made them feel worthwhile and beautiful about themselves.

Oprah Winfrey became a mother to millions all over the world. She became a girlfriend to women who needed assurance and comfort from their painful pasts. She became a grandmother to little girls who looked up to her for courage, inspiration, and hope. Oprah showed us all that if we believe in ourselves, anything is possible.

"The greatest discovery of all time is that a person can change his future by merely changing his attitude."

Victoria Woodhull

First American Woman to Run for President

Victoria Woodhull started the first female-owned American company in the business of buying and selling stocks. She also became the first woman to run for President in 1872. Some 140 years later, she still remains ahead of her time.

- Born on September 23, 1838
- In 1871, she became the first woman in history to address a committee of the U.S. congress.
- In 1872, she became the first woman to run for president.
- Fought for women's rights
- Died on June 9, 1927

From poverty to prosperity...from nothing to everything: Victoria Woodhull overcame the impossible to become the first woman to run for President in America. It was unthinkable in 1872. Physical, emotional, financial, and sexual exhaustion dotted her entire life. She found little solace in the men that entered and occasionally exited her life, and she tirelessly worked for the rights of women. Victoria used her abilities to communicate with dead people and preaching to take her to the top rungs of society. This talent for making prophesies culminated in her meeting with Cornelius Vanderbilt, the richest man in America at the time. It was all because she nurtured a simple character trait: stop talking and listen.

Birth and Family Poverty

Victoria Claflin was born in Homer, Ohio, in 1838. She was the seventh of ten children. At mealtimes the children roamed to other houses to beg for food. She was raised by a physically abusive father. Buck Claflin was neither a parent nor a particularly kind man. When his children displeased him, he beat them. As Victoria would recall many years later, her father "was impartial in his cruelty to all his children. I have no remembrance of a father's kisses." She vaguely understood that they were barely staying afloat in a sea of economic worries. In spite of their difficulties, or maybe because of them, the Claflins developed a very strong sense of family loyalty. Though they may have fought between themselves, when criticized by outsiders, they defended one another fiercely.

Victoria's father was a con artist and petty criminal. Yet, he told his daughter, "Girl, your worth has never yet been known, but to the world it shall be shown." He also gave her a piece of practical advice: "Be a good listener, child." Victoria took that advice to heart.

Victoria's early education consisted of a total of three years of elementary school, which she attended off and on between ages eight and eleven. She was a "child without a childhood." She had been farmed out as "a household drudge" to begin at dawn on endless rounds of washing and ironing, running errands, spading gardens, chopping wood, laying fires, and tending infants.

It was a bleak life, and Victoria dreamed of something different. She always thought big, and allowed herself to dream one size bigger. When they were shunned by their more respectable neighbors, her mother told her girls that they were "different" and what she did, or what they did, was right simply because they did it. She told them that God was within them, and so any action they took could not be wrong. This feeling of entitlement was to persist throughout Victoria's long life.

At age eight, she used her singing voice to become a child preacher. She narrated Bible stories from atop a mound, which she called the "Mount of Olives." It was on that mound that she experienced the thrill of audience approval. Even in her youth she was a consummate showman, addicted to attention.

Communicating with Spirits

Unable to protect herself from the parents who enslaved her emotionally, abused and exhausted, this child-woman retreated to a safe world. She conversed daily with her two dead sisters, Delia and Odessa: "I would talk to them as a girl talks to her dolls," she said. Victoria believed that the spirits guarded and sustained her.

Victoria and her sister Tennessee charged people for their spiritual healing. They were the primary breadwinners in the Claflin family, supporting their extended clan, which, rather than thanking them for their efforts, jealously resented their success. Victoria became a green leaf and her legions of relatives were caterpillars that devoured her.

"I think a woman is just as capable of making a living as a man."

Flawed Teen Marriage

Canning Woodhull of Rochester, New York, claimed to be a doctor. He also claimed to be the son of a judge and the nephew of the mayor of New York City. His path crossed Victoria Claflin's when he was called by her family to treat her fever and rheumatism. In 1853, when Victoria was fifteen years old, they married. In marrying her doctor, Victoria may have seen herself as one of the heroines glamorized in popular fiction; a damsel rescued from poverty and illness by a handsome, rich doctor. "My marriage was an escape," she said.

The young bride soon discovered that her husband was not the son of a judge, nor had he ever met the mayor of New York. She also learned that her husband had no real medical practice and, therefore, no steady income. What he did have was a battery of bad habits, including frequenting houses of ill repute. He was also an alcoholic and a morphine addict.

Talking about her flawed first marriage, Victoria Woodhull said, "In a single day I grew ten years older.... The shock awoke all my womanhood." Victoria's marriage robbed her of her childhood.

According to Victoria's highly colored account, Canning had not shared her bed since the third night of their marriage. After only six weeks of marriage, she found that he was fathering another baby that he had by another woman. He slept at the local brothel. When the money ran out and she went to look for him, following his trail from tavern to tavern, she finally found him eating pigeon pie and drinking champagne at brothels. At night, she would stand by the window waiting. Sometimes in the early morning hours, she heard the faltering steps of her husband as he stumbled along the cobblestones, having been drunk all night.

In the winter of 1854, Victoria, attended by her "half drunken" husband, gave birth to a son. It was a long and painful delivery. He left her right around the time the baby was born to be with his girlfriend. The son, Byron, never developed teeth and his speech was never more than a series of grunts. Sometimes, Victoria said, Byron was born challenged because Canning had kicked her in the stomach while she was pregnant. At other times she said that as an infant, Byron had fallen from a second story window. Sometimes, she blamed herself. Victoria still believed that marriage was a sacred institution and she "wrestled" with God to find a way to live with this arrangement.

Victoria slowly began to understand that she could not depend on her husband. Maybe she could never depend on any man. In the future, she would have to take care of herself, her baby, and yes, also her husband. If he would not be the head of their family, as tradition demanded, then the position went to her by default. In April 1861, her daughter Zulu Maud was born healthy and beautiful.

Listening to Others and Making Money

Along with Tennessee, Victoria traveled from town to town as a fortune teller and healer. The Claflins rode in caravan style in the tortured fields of recent battles in the Civil War. The war was nearly over and there was plenty of misery everywhere they traveled. Much of the blood spilled on the paths the Claflins traveled. They sold hope to the hopeless in the form of sham medicine and mysterious revelations. Among the diseases the family promised to cure was diphtheria, heart and liver complaints, asthma, fits, cancer within twenty-four hours, loss of sight or hearing, and all problems "pertaining to life and health." They also offered to communicate with dead spirits, find lost items, and generally sort out domestic problems of all types.

During these travels Victoria encountered thousands of stories of broken men and women who sought her advice on loveless and abusive marriages that they were too terrified to end. She listened to the stories of women who confided they were forced to endure sexual relations and bear children by men they detested. She met women who were driven into prostitution after being abandoned by men to whom they had given themselves in trust. The Claflins made thousands of dollars by listening to other people's woes.

It was also during these travels that Victoria met and married Colonel James Harvey Blood, a war veteran. Blood was an advocate of new and fresh thinking. He supported women's rights and social freedom for all and set about introducing Victoria to the reform doctrines. It took a year for their marriage to get legalized as she was still married to Canning Woodhull. With James Harvey Blood, Victoria had a partner who not only shared the burdens of everyday life with her, but who reawakened her intellect as well.

On a temporary sojourn to Pittsburgh, Victoria was sitting in the parlor of a boardinghouse when a spirit in a white toga came to her and said: "Your work is about to begin. All these years you have been preparing for a great mission. Go to New York City, to 17 Great Jones Street. There you will find a house ready and waiting for you and yours." Then a vision of a house willed with comfortable furniture floated before her eyes. She followed the vision. Victoria moved her family to New York. It was 1868; the year that changed her life.

Meeting the Richest Man in America

The vision paved the way for a meeting with Cornelius Vanderbilt, who was seventy-three years old and the richest man in America at the time. He detested doctors and ministers. Vanderbilt experienced visions, believed in Spiritualism, and instructed his barber to collect his hair and burn it out of fear that someone who secured a lock of it would have power over him. When the 73-year-old's joints ached, he consulted a spiritual healer who could relieve his pain by "laying on of hands." Rather than attend church, he visited a psychic on Staten Island who brought him messages from his dead mother.

Victoria put Vanderbilt in touch with his dead mother and offered financial advice. She predicted about a stock that would go up. Vanderbilt was so amused by her that one day he said he would split the profits if her next stock tip proved right…. It did, and Victoria Woodhull was suddenly rich.

Financially armed, Victoria turned her fight to women's rights and responsibilities. She set about promoting her vision of equal rights by example. There were no women on Wall Street. By focusing on finance and taking her place in the male bastion of the stock market, Victoria earned instant notoriety.

"When I first came to Wall Street, not 100 women in the whole of the United States owned stocks or dared to show independence in property ownership. For a woman to consider a financial question was shuddered over as a profanity," she noted.

Woodhull, Claflin, & Co.

Victoria and Tennessee formed Woodhull, Claflin, & Co., the first female-owned American company in the business of buying and selling stocks.

On February 5, 1870, Woodhull, Claflin, & Co. formally opened its doors to the public. It was a brokerage firm. In a front-page story, the *New York Sun* read that change had come to Wall Street with the headline: "Petticoats Among the Bovine and Ursine Animals." At the stock and gold exchanges, the news of a brokerage firm operated by women was greeted with a frenzy of speculation. The presence on Wall Street of Victoria Woodhull and her sister Tennessee Claflin created a commotion only slightly less dramatic than a crash. From early morning until the business closed, males crowded the sidewalks outside their office. They were peeking at the female broker.

It was a historic moment. It would be another century before a woman would hold a seat in her own name on the New York Stock Exchange, and possibly never again would a pair of female financiers cause such a stir. Businesses in the area closed their doors and hurried over to see what was going on. Four thousand people had thronged through the offices. The press called them all sorts of names: "the bewitching brokers" and "the she-brokers."

The opening of Woodhull, Claflin, & Co., was a crucial step toward Victoria's goal. It provided the financial backing she needed to thrust her into public spotlight, where she would begin her crusade for women's rights.

The official opening of Woodhull, Clafllin & Co., was announced in both the stock and gold exchanges. Traders sang songs and made jokes at the expense of the fair newcomers who dared to breach the masculine fortress of Wall Street. Many speculated over their potential impact on the market. In less than four months, Victoria had gone from being just another obscure woman, living on the edge of financial ruin with only her wits to help her survive, to being in a position of prominence and wealth in the greatest metropolis in the United States. The family moved into a fashionable mansion.

Speaker, Suffragist... Presidential Candidate

Victoria began speaking out at women's rights meetings. Leading suffragists admired her efforts: Susan B. Anthony hailed her as a "bright, glorious, young and strong spirit" while Elizabeth Cady Stanton praised the "work for women that none of us could have done." Later, however, their relationships would sour.

Victoria Woodhull was forced into a first marriage at age fifteen to a man twice her age. Since then, she had vowed to become a leader in the fight for women's rights. She was determined that no woman should be forced to endure her early heartache, to offer her body, in marriage or on the street, in exchange for financial security. For Victoria the fight for women's equality was not simply a matter of gaining access to the ballot box — it was a matter of winning the basic right of self ownership.

Women could not vote, but Victoria found out one day that no laws kept them out of public office. The only way a woman could hope to compete was to nominate herself, so in 1870 she did the unthinkable. She sent this notice to the *New York Herald*: "I now announce myself as a candidate for the Presidency." No woman had ever been elected to Congress, let alone the White House. In 1871 she became the first woman in history to address a committee of the U.S. Congress. Victoria realized her campaign was doomed unless women could vote for her, so, on a national speaking tour a year into her campaign, she became the first woman in history to address Congress. All the major newspapers covered Victoria's speech. President Ulysses S. Grant invited her to the White House and reportedly told her she might occupy his office someday.

"While others prayed for the good time coming, I worked for it," Victoria said.

At thirty-two years old, Victoria declared herself a candidate for president of the United States. In the days after her announcement, Victoria's presidential candidacy was treated as a novelty by the press. Victoria was treated as a pet. For the moment, the power brokers on Wall Street and in the press were happy to let her have her fun. "I have deliberately, and of my own accord, placed myself before the people as a candidate for the Presidency of the United States, and having the means, courage, energy, and strength necessary for the race, intend to contest it to the close."

During the next local election, she and Tennessee led a group of women to a polling booth. The men at the polling booth laughed at the women. Victoria gave a stirring speech about a women's right to vote. After the failed voting attempt, the media began to belittle her campaign.

Victoria believed very strongly in herself. Her vision also insisted that she would lead her people. In those days some unlikely people had become President. Where had Abraham Lincoln been before his nomination? A self-educated country lawyer who had become an Illinois State Legislator. Certainly the notion of a woman President sounded strange, but no woman had ever tried it before.

Victoria had no political party behind her and no political experience to support her claim that she was a serious candidate. It was the most outrageous act she could dream up to prove women's equality. She had two years to build a campaign that would get people to take her seriously.

"While others of my sex devoted themselves to a crusade against the laws that shackle the women of the country, I asserted my individual independence; while others prayed for the god time coming, I worked for it; while others argued the equality of women with man, I proved it by successfully engaging in business; while others sought to show that there was no valid reason why women should be treated, socially and politically, as being inferior to man, I boldly entered the arena... of business and exercised the rights I already possessed...I therefore claim the right to speak for the enfranchised women of the country, and believing as I do that the prejudices which still exist in the popular mind against women in public life will soon disappear, I now announce myself as candidate for the Presidency."

Woodhull & Claflin's Weekly

Victoria and Tennessee founded their own newspaper, *Woodhull & Claflin's Weekly*, and used it to voice Victoria's positions on the country's problems. Over the months, *Woodhull & Claflin's Weekly* gradually became more radical. Women could still read about a female contractor in New Hampshire or a postmistress at West Point, but the paper also began to expose insurance frauds and bond swindles. *Woodhull & Claflin's Weekly* was the first American publication to reprint the Communist Manifesto. It was not a women's paper, a financial paper, or a political paper. Rather, it was all of these things. It perfectly lit her belief that in order to move forward toward increased rights for women and a generally healthier society, the various interest groups must unite. She was now a publisher, not the first or only woman to own her own newspaper, but certainly one of the few.

"All this talk about women's rights is moonshine. Women have every right. All they need to do is exercise them. That's what we are doing. We are doing more for women's rights by being here on Wall Street than all the speeches will do in ten years."

Victoria used the proceeds from her brokerage business to attack in print and on the lecture circuit the hypocrisy and corruption she found in the world of politics, finance, and religion. She became the most notorious and polarizing woman of her day.

Her Presidential Campaign

The next election would not be until 1872. She would need two years to establish herself. She had to reeducate the men of the country, the ones who cast the ballots. Very, very few men approved of women in public life. They believed women belonged in the home, preferably in the kitchen. Most women agreed. The great political parties did not take women seriously. After all, a woman couldn't even vote. A woman on the ticket would be more than a liability. It would be a joke.

Looking back, Victoria's campaign must be rated as one of the most carefully thought out in American political history. She did everything right, up to a point, that is. Announcing her candidacy was only the first step. She had no intention of stopping there. People already knew that she was a wealthy, self made woman. Now she had to make the entire country aware of the socialist principles for which she stood.

She began to write a series of essays about politics and government that later would be published as a book, *The Principles of Government*. The essays, appearing first in the *New York Herald*, were much too scholarly for the average reader, but they succeeded in giving Victoria a new image. People couldn't help but conclude that Mrs. Woodhull was a learned woman, a person who had the intelligence and qualifications to be president.

Some newspapers pointed out that she was a smart and handsome woman. Therefore, "she is the proper person to stand forth against the field as the woman's rights candidate for the White House." Others, however, sneered. The "weaker sex," they said, already have enough privileges. Women should be happy with what they have. The obvious was mentioned; that men would never accept a woman president. Any man believed that it was unnatural for a woman to govern.

As news of Victoria's candidacy traveled across the country, people began to talk about her. Men asked what the world was coming to. Some felt sure that she must be a homely, man eating spinster with a cat. Only that type of woman would make a public spectacle of herself. Other men said she must be a beautiful courtesan. Only that type of woman would call attention to herself.

Over their teacups, the women also gossiped about her. Victoria intrigued them. They wanted to know all about her but what they learned made them feel uneasy. She might be rich and beautiful, but she also sounded "unfeminine." No true woman would demean herself by running for political office. This woman troubled them.

How She was Ostracized

On January 11, 1871, Victoria addressed the House Judiciary Committee in Washington. She began to read her speech: "Women, White and Black, belong to races, although to different races. A race of people comprises all the people, male and female." Her sincere passion and an intense belief in the truth of her argument came across strongly to the audience. "The right to vote cannot be denied on account of race. Neither does sex have anything to do with the right to vote."

The involvement with exposing Henry Ward Beecher's affair did not go well with Victoria's run for presidency. Henry Beecher was a prominent preacher, earning good money at the time. Later on Susan B. Anthony would move away from Victoria, as she felt that Victoria was turning the women suffrage movement into a political party for her own ends. Things began to turn sour for her. Her landlord asked her to move out.

For several weeks afterwards, Victoria, Blood, and family members slept on the floor of their brokerage office. She felt the Beecher family was behind all of it. Many lies spread about her.

There was another reason for the ostracism: Victoria Woodhull was a woman.

On the morning of 1872, a bundle of five hundred copies of the *Woodhull & Claflin Weekly* were distributed to a newsstand on the busy corner of Broad and Wall Streets. They sold right away. The lead article on Beecher, written by Victoria herself, ran eleven columns. She justified her attack on the minister Henry Beecher in the name of social revolution. In effect, she told her readers that they can't make scrambled eggs without breaking a few eggshells. "The fault with which I therefore charge him is not infidelity to the old ideas, but unfaithfulness to the new.… It is nobody's business but their own what Mr. Beecher and Mrs. Tilton have done, as between themselves."

She clearly understood that men, especially powerful men like Henry Beecher, had the freedom to flout society's rules. They could practice "free love" in secret and get away with it. A woman could not. The unfair double standard, against which she had fought for so many years, finally caught up with her. Any woman rash enough to defy the rules that kept women in their place was bound to be punished sooner or later.

Harder Times Ahead

On election day, November 5, 1872, when she should have been focused on her presidential bid, Victoria was imprisoned in New York City on a charge of sending obscene material through the mail. She was left discredited, bankrupt, and abandoned. Her name was completely left out of historical writing in the early women's movement, Victoria herself identified the reason — she was ahead of her time.

Victoria Woodhull did not, of course, win the 1872 election. Ulysses S. Grant won. Victoria did not even get to try to vote for herself. "To be perfectly frank, I hardly expected to be elected. The truth is I am too many years ahead of this age…and the unenlightened mind of the average man."

The year 1873 became more difficult. Victoria was put in jail. Money was tight. They had to use streetcars to get around New York City rather than traveling in chauffeur-driven carriages.

Death

Victoria moved to England, where she was finally able to earn proper respect from society. To avoid germs she refused to shake hands or be kissed. Visitors were permitted to come no closer than six feet. She ordered her drinking water boiled. On the morning of June 10, 1927, at 2 a.m., death visited her. Victoria Woodhull left instructions that she be cremated and her ashes cast into the sea. She willed her fortune to Zulu, her daughter, who never married, having devoted her life to her mother.

A month before her death, she scrawled what might have been her epitaph:

"The deeper I delve for a sure footing, the higher I reach for light, the more convinced am I that only here and there do we find an instrument capable of responding to the hungry heart's desire for Truth…On the retina of our brain the outline of Truth is revealed to those attuned to the music of the spheres… Therefore I feel well assured that whatever be the misrepresentations to which I may be subject, the events must be committed to tie, who relentlessly unravels all distortions and rights all wrongs…Whoever I am, whatever I have done, belongs to the sprits."

In 1927, eight years after women finally won the right to vote, Victoria Woodhull died at the age of eighty-nine, a forgotten figure.

The Strides She Made

Victoria Woodhull sincerely believed that all women benefited from seeing one of their gender enter a male arena. In taking on the business world, publishing, religion, and politics, all the male-dominated institutions of her day, she broke many boundaries. Society punished her harshly. "If my political campaign for Presidency is not successful, it will be educational."

Even though society misunderstood her, within her heart, she felt right about her life. Victoria Woodhull was the Spiritualist, the "high priestess" of free love, the crusading editor, the founder of the first stock brokerage firm for women, the disciple of Karl Marx, the presidential candidate, the sinner, the saint. She had been all of these and more, for in her many aspects, she combined in abundance many of the influences that shaped the women of her world.

The time for a Victoria Woodhull still lies somewhere over the horizon. Someday soon, there will be a skirt in the White House and Victoria Woodhull gets the credit for setting the foundation for that day.

Bartley, Paula. *Emmeline Pankhurst*. Routledge, London and New York: Routledge, 2002.

Benenate, Becky and Joseph Durepos, Editors. *No Greater Love: Mother Teresa*. California: New World Library, 2002.

Blashfield, Jean F. *Women at the Front: Their Changing Roles in the Civil War*. New York, New York: Franklin Watts, 1997.

Bundles, A'Lelia. *On Her Own Ground: The Life and Times of Madam C.J. Walker*. New York, New York: Lisa Drew Books, 2002.

Burns, Bree. *Harriet Tubman and the Fight Against Slavery*. New York, New York: Chelsea House Publishers, 1992.

Colligan, Victoria, and Beth Schoenfeldt. *Ladies Who Launch*. New York: St. Martin's Press, 2007.

Clements, Alan. *The Voice of Hope: Aung San Suu Kyi*. New York: Seven Stories Press, 2008.

Cooper, Ilene. *Up Close: Oprah Winfrey*. New York, New York: Viking Children's Books, 2007.

Dobler, Lavinia, *Esther Morris: First Woman Justice of the Peace*. Riverton, Wyoming: Big Bend Press, 1993.

Elish, Dan. Harriet Tubman and the Underground Railroad. Connecticut: Millbrook Press, 1993.

Feldman, Heather. *Valentina Tereshkova: The First Woman in Space*. New York, New York: Rosen Publishing Group, 2003.

Gabriel, Mary. *Notorious Victoria: The Life of Victoria Woodhull, Uncensored*. Chapel Hill, North Carolina: Algonquin Books, 1998.

Golden, Kristen, and Barbara Findlen. *Remarkable Women of the Twentieth Century*. New York, New York: Friedman Fairfax Publishers, 1998.

Goldsmith, Barbara. *Obsessive Genius: The Inner World of Marie Curie*. New York, New York: W. W. Norton & Company, 2005.
Other Powers: The Age of Suffrage, Spiritualism, and the Scandalous Victoria Woodhull. New York: Alfred Knopf, 1998.

Goldsmith, Marshall. *What Got you Here Won't get you There*. Self-published, 2007.

Gulatta, Charles. *Extraordinary Women in Politics*. New York: Children's Press, 1998.

Harper, Judith E. *Susan B. Anthony: A Biographical Companion.* Santa Barbara, California: ABC-CLIO, 1998.

Head, Judith. *America's Daughters: 400 Years of American Women.* Los Angeles, California: Perspective Publishing, 1999.

Jones, Victoria Garrett. *Amelia Earhart: A Life in Flight.* New York, New York: Sterling Publishing Co., 2009.

Krull, Kathleen. *A Woman for President: The Story of Victoria Woodhull.* New York: Walker Publishing, 2004.

Krull, Kathleen and David Diaz. *Wilma Unlimited: How Wilma Rudolph Became the World's Fastest Woman.* New York: Harcourt Brace & Company, 1996.

Langford, Joseph. *Mother Teresa's Secret Fire.* Huntington, Indiana: Our Sunday Publishing Division, 2008.

Lawrence, Regina G. and Melody Rose. *Hillary Clinton's Race for the White House: Gender Politics & the Media on the Campaign Trail.* Boulder, Colorado: Lynne Rienner Publishers, 2010.

Ling, Bettina. *Aung San Suu Kyi: Standing Up for Democracy in Burma.* New York, New York: University of New York, 1999.

Long, Elgen M. and Marie K. Long. *Amelia Earhart.* New York, New York: Simon and Schuster, 1999.

Lovell, Mary S. *The Life of Amelia Earhart: The Sound of Wings.* New York: St. Martin's Press, 1989.

Maxwell, John C. *How Successful People Think.* New York: Center Street, 2009.

McClafferty, Carla Killough. *Something out of Nothing: Marie Curie and Radiation.* New York, New York: Carla Killough McClafferty, 2006.

Meade, Marion. *Free Woman: Life of Victoria Woodhull.* New York, New York: Alfred Knopf, 1976.

Owry, Beverly. *Her Dream of Dreams.* New York, New York: Random House, 2003.

Pankhurst, E. Sylvia. *The Life of Emmeline Pankhurst.* London: T. Werner Laurie Ltd., 1969.

Pankhurst, Emmeline. *My Own Story.* London: Source Book Press, 1914

Pinkey, Andrea Davis. *Let it Shine: Stories of Black Women Freedom Fighters.* New York, New York: Gulliver Books, 2000.

Purvis, June. *Emmeline Pankhurst: A Biography*. London and New York: Routledge, 2002.

Raatma, Lucia. *Leading Women: Shirley Chisholm*. New York: Marshall Cavendish Corporation, 2011.

Rappaport, Doreen. *Eleanor: Quiet No More: The Life of Eleanor Roosevelt*. New York: Hyperion Books, 2009.

Roosevelt, Eleanor. *The Autobiography of Eleanor Roosevelt*. New York: Da Capo Press, 1992.

Shalit, Willa. *Becoming Myself, Reflections on Growing up Female*. New York: Hyperion, 2006.

Shayler, David J. and Ian Moule. *Women in Space Following Valentina*. United Kingdom: Praxis Publishing, 2005.

Steele, Philip. *Marie Curie: The Woman Who Changed the Course of Science*. Washington D.C.: National Geographic Society, 2006.

Tichler, Rosemarie, and Barry Jay Caplin. *Actors at Work*. New York: Faber and Faber, 2007.

Wintle, Justin. *Perfect Hostage: A Life of Aung San Suu Kyi, Burma's Prisoner of Conscience*. Great Britain: Kutchinson, 2007.

Wooldridge, Connie Nordhielm. When Esther Morris Headed West. New York: Holiday House, 2001.

Wright, Vinita Hampton. *Simple Acts of Moving Forward*. Colorado Springs, Colorado: Shaw Books, 2003.